GREAT ASIA STEAMBOOK

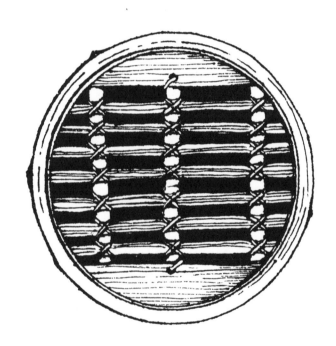

BY IRENE WONG

To

Alan Gribben

who recognizes good ideas

Photography by Nadine Ohara
Cover photos by David Fischer

ISBN 0-912738-11-1

Library of Congress Card 77-89302
Printed in the United States of America
Copyright © 1977 by Irene Wong
Published by Taylor & Ng
P.O. Box 200
Brisbane, California 94005
    All Rights Reserved
    First Edition
    Second Printing
Distributed by Random House, Inc.
and in Canada by Random House of Canada, Ltd.
ISBN 394-73563-3

ABOUT THE AUTHOR

Irene Wong represents the emerging generation of young professional women with Chinese-American backgrounds. Born in Fresno, California in 1949, Irene grew up in a spacious Victorian frame house in the thriving Chinatown section. She participated in local festivals and banquets, and came to know most of the Chinese and Japanese families who settled in the agricultural towns of the San Joaquin Valley, a land of irrigated fig, orange, almond, and olive orchards; grape vineyards; and raisin and wine industries. Her father and uncle had immigrated from Sun Doh, a village in the Kwangtung province of mainland China, when the Japanese army invaded the region in 1938. In Fresno the brothers owned and operated in succession a hotel, a restaurant named Dragon Cafe, a department store, and two grocery stores. Their families inhabited a transplanted Chinese village of uncles, aunts, cousins, grandparents, and Chinese neighbors, all of whom tended a communal garden that stretched behind their adjacent houses. As a young girl, Irene took her turn watering and harvesting the *bok choy*, Chinese peanuts, winter melons, and other vegetables.

Irene's mother, Jean Chin Wong, initially discouraged Irene and her older sister Lorraine from learning how to cook, insisting that they'd have plenty of time to master the craft after they were married. Fortunately Irene was adept at observing her mother's greaseless stir-frying and steaming techniques and making mental notes. She first began cooking while attending the University of California at Berkeley; there she astonished her fiancé and his friends by preparing six- and eight-course meals. After graduating from the university, Irene taught English as a second language in the Chinatown of nearby Oakland.

In 1974 she married Alan Gribben, now an assistant English professor at the University of Texas in Austin. Eventually Irene met a woman whose cooking techniques agreed with her own, Rhoda Yee, author of *Chinese Village Cookbook* (1975). Advised by Rhoda, Irene began teaching classes in using the wok.

Currently Irene is a Chinese-cooking instructor for Taylor & Ng, San Francisco importers and designers; she travels throughout the South and Southwest. Irene punctuates her culinary demonstrations with anecdotes drawn from her cultural heritage. Although she has appeared in Phoenix, Las Vegas, St. Louis, Tampa, Orlando, and other cities, she teaches most frequently in Dallas, Austin, and San Antonio. *Texas Monthly Magazine* called her a "gem" of an instructor, praising her participation-method of teaching and noting that her students are "mad enthusiasts."

To write *The Great Asia Steambook*, Irene investigated Oriental steaming practices that prevail in the Eastern hemisphere from India to Polynesia, from Malaysia to China to Japan. Her book collects the recipes of her far-flung family and friends as well as the results of her kitchen experiments.

Table of Contents

Preface

Asian steam cookery — as old as Eastern civilization, yet unchanged even today — preserves the vitamins and flavors in foods, adds no fats, generally takes less than an hour, saves money since it consolidates all cooking on one water-covered heat source (which also makes cleaning up easy — no scouring, ever!), and combines with stir-frying, braising, and other cooking methods to produce scores of variations on basic recipes.

When the huge English and American steamships visited ports of call in Hawaii, Indonesia, India, Thailand, China, and Japan at the turn of the century, their passengers sampled exotic entreés and desserts steamed in bamboo baskets or leaves. For centuries, these peoples of Asia, the South Pacific, and Southeast Asia had been steaming their foods. Nowadays, steaming still accounts for more than half of home-cooking in China. A single pot of boiling water with a tier of stacking bamboo-woven or aluminum trays cooks all the meat, rice, and vegetables at one time. The liquid underneath can be a soup that itself produces the steam.

The Pacific islanders originally steamed their foods, although they lacked the metal cooking utensils that Asia used. Whenever they cooked (though they seldom did, and only for feasts) they dug an underground oven to be filled with heated rocks, a stuffed pig, leaf-wrapped vegetables and fish, and covered with banana leaves and more hot stones. There was no water in the oven, but the heat from the rocks caused the moisture in the *ti* and banana leaves to steam the wrapped butterfish, bananas, taro, and breadfruit.

The people of India sometimes steamed foods in their brass pans by caulking around the lid and the pot with a flour and water mixture. This *dum* cooking simmered and steamed dishes in a little water.

What *is* steam cooking? To Asians, it's usually "wet steaming" — permitting steam vapor to envelop and heat the food. "Dry steaming" also cooks with steam, but the water vapor doesn't touch the food (like melting chocolate in a double boiler). Steam can be thought of as a hot gas produced by vigorously boiling water. It cooks food without burning it. Steam is actually invisible; the cloud we see is water that condenses as the steam cools in the outer air. A steamer — aluminum, bamboo, or steel — effectively contains the steam and its pressure. Today steam cookery is easier than ever, since we don't need to build fires or underground ovens to produce our steam. Using a stove top, we can employ one burner to generate enough steam to cook an entire meal in 30 minutes. This saves fuel, time, and preparation. And steaming really is the simplest way to cook: one merely assembles the ingredients and clocks the outcome.

This cookbook tours the Asian countries where steaming is most popular. The steamed-food recipes retain the natural flavors of fish, chicken, and pork, but also add piquant sauces. The results range from the Crispy Onion Fish of Malaysia to the tasty Spareribs in Black Bean Sauce of China.

Steamed recipes are best appreciated when they contrast with other methods of cooking: the stir-fried meats of Vietnam, the curry stews of India, the broiled shrimp of Japan. Sometimes the steaming method is combined with other methods such as boiling and deep-frying to create the crispy and tender Almond Pressed Duck.

In recipes, at least, it's still possible to travel back a century to the other side of the world when sleek steamships docked at tropical isles, explored faraway countries, and sought exotic cuisines. Start with Kwangtung Fish, a basic but infallible dish, or Rice Cakes, an easy dessert, and bring the pleasures of steam cooking into your kitchen.

the art & tools of steaming

ALUMINUM & BAMBOO STEAMERS

Most Chinese, Japanese, Vietnamese, Malaysian, and Indonesian homes use either the multi-layered bamboo or else aluminum baskets; a lid on the top tray prevents the steam from escaping. These racks sit on top of a wok which holds enough water to steam half an hour. Aluminum steamers consist of a pot, one or two racks, and a lid. A nine-quart pot with two 12-inch trays handles an entire meal: meat, rice, and two or three vegetable or meat side-dishes. Look for a high-sided steamer with a domed lid so you can cook a whole chicken in it if you wish.

Aluminum retains the heat better than bamboo, cooks more dishes faster, and doesn't pick up pungent odors when one steams shrimp and crab in their shells. Aluminum steamers don't mildew or split, and thus are a permanent addition to every kitchen. In sum, the aluminum steamer (with its deep pot and metal trays) is more efficient, though the bamboo ones are ethnic and colorful. The woven tops and banded sides of the bamboo trays absorb and leak steam that the metal ones contain and cook with. The average bamboo steamer is 10 inches in diameter and accommodates only an 8-inch plate or small bowls. But I like to steam dumplings in bamboo because some of the moisture is absorbed into the bamboo and consequently the dough feels less damp and gooey.

When you buy bamboo trays (mine are almost 10 years old), wet them thoroughly at first and heat them as you would for cooking except don't put any food inside. Steam for an hour, replenishing water as necessary and pouring water over the trays to keep them moist. This initial curing removes the acrid bamboo smell that otherwise would transfer to the foods. With more use, the trays age and the bamboo retains a faint but pleasant scent. Keep the trays out on the counter as a decorative kitchen utensil — this is the best protection against mildew. Don't cover them with plastic wrap.

STEAMING PROCEDURES

When cooking, you may set steamed dumplings and wrapped fish directly on the trays. (A brush scrubs off any dough that sticks to the bamboo.) But it's best to line aluminum and bamboo trays with a wet cotton cloth before laying truly sticky tidbits on them. Place unwrapped meats and vegetables on a plate so that none of their juices (and vitamins) drain through the slats or holes of the baskets. Be sure to bring the water to a boil before you set the dish on the tray. At that point you begin to time the cooking period. But don't get burned in the process.

To place food in a steamer, or retrieve it when finished without getting a painful steam burn, use a pair of cook's mitts that cover the forearms. Take off the lid (tipping it *away* from you), let the steam dissipate, then take the dish out with both covered hands — or move the entire steaming tray off the pot and cautiously remove the plate. If you ever forget these precautions and have your hand above the escaping steam vapor, run cold tap water on the burned area until the pain decreases — and begin this treatment immediately (the sooner the better). For severe cases, a dishtowel soaked with water and filled with ice cubes lowers the skin temperature of the affected region and allows the pain to subside. With a little care, however, steam cooking is really less dangerous than the grease-splattering methods of other modes of food preparation.

1

BAMBOO STEAMER:

ALTERNATIVE STEAMERS

When making do with a deep pot, use a one or two-pound coffee can with both ends cut out. Rest the plate of food on top of this. You can use a tea towel around the lid to absorb any water that might drip into the food. The best conductors of heat are clear glass plates or dishes and metal pie pans. A decorated heat-proof platter can also be used; it shows off vegetables attractively when served. I transfer food from the steaming utensil to a heated plate; the meal cools too fast on an unheated one.

ELECTRIC SKILLET:

The most convenient substitute for an Oriental steamer is an electric skillet. Place a heatproof

ashtray (3-inches high), canning ring, or a small tuna can with both ends removed to act as a trivet in the middle of the skillet. Set a plate of raw food on top of the platform. Make sure that the plate does not touch the sides of the pan — an inch from the sides all around is sufficient for the steam to rise, circulate, and cook the food. Open the air vent on the lid so that water vapor won't drip into the plate.

If you have a wok but no stacking trays, you can invent stands — a cake cooling rack, circular metal hot plates, or two pieces of wood (notched in the center of each piece and fitted together) across the bowl of the wok work well. Add water but not enough to reach the bottom of the dish or it might boil over into the food. (If you need to add water while the dish is cooking, use the hottest water from the tap or else boiling water, since they reach steaming temperatures sooner.) Cover with a high-domed lid.

PRESSURE COOKER:

A pressure cooker is an excellent steamer. It cuts the steaming time for whole chickens and ducks from two hours to half an hour. You would not need a plate in a pressure cooker. Set the pressure at 15 pounds per square inch for meats.

OCCIDENTAL & MORE ORIENTAL STEAMERS

There are several types of Occidental and other Oriental steamers on the market. In general, they are smaller and suitable for one or two people. These include:

A stainless steaming basket that has holes all over it and fits into different size pans by expanding or folding. There is a stem with a ring to lift the tray; unfortunately this post prevents one's placing a dish on the tray. But the basket fits inside a bamboo or aluminum rack.

A six-quart pot with a two-quart insert. There are holes around the rim of the smaller pot and these let steam in for wet steaming at least one recipe.

An automatic rice cooker and steamer manufactured in the Orient. The perforated steaming tray allows the steam to pass through. An inch of water placed in the removable pot lasts 15 minutes. Small bowls and custard cups do not tip over in this utensil.

An ironstone steamer that is bowl-shaped and covered. A chimney in the middle acts as a tunnel for the steam to enter the bowl from a pot of boiling water underneath. The bowl rests on any two-quart pot and acts as a serving dish, too. This utensil styled after steamers used in Yunnan Province, China gently cooks fish and soups.

A clam and lobster enamel steamer with a pot, one tray and a flat lid. It is best for unwrapped foods. A plate covers most of the holes and prevents the steam from rising.

A six-quart stainless pot with a wire basket and domed lid. This deep-fryer would be ideal to cook a fish Japanese style — the fish can be cooked uncovered and basted with its own juices that drain through the wire basket.

An electric steamer with cooking bowls — some partitioned — that stack above the heating element and the boiling water.

MINCE, MEAT, & THE CLEAVER

Orientals always judge texture critically — the smoothness of an egg custard, the delicate flakiness of a cooked fish, the softness of minced meats. Grinding instead of mincing meat is a quick way to prepare large quantities to fill won tons for frying, but it isn't acceptable for true minced-meat dishes. Whereas mincing produces the light, airy texture of pureé, varied by little bits of meat to chew, steamed ground meats feel uniformly compact and dry. Mincing — especially with two cleavers — quickly reduces strips of pork, chicken, or beef to a patty. The movement of this chopping and the muffled sound of the cleaver touching wood relaxes people listening hungrily for the noises of kitchen activity.

Many steamed dishes require minced ingredients. These suggestions may assist you.

1. Two cleavers are faster than one since you use both hands and keep a rhythm. When you pause, scrape one blade against the other, then group the minced patty and mince again.

2. Remember that larger quantities are easier to mince than small ones (such as a clove of garlic). Whenever possible, first coarsely slice water chestnuts, ginger, green onions, ginger slices, chili peppers, or coriander leaves. Then make a mound of those to be combined and mince them all at one time.

3. When mincing two meats, slice the individual meats in long strips, then cut crosswise. Bring the meats together and mince with two cleavers. Chicken and pork are good combinations, but mince shrimp separately since it is so soft that it becomes a paste rather quickly.

STEAMING TIMES TO CALL YOUR OWN

Cooking times for steamed recipes vary, depending on whether the dish sets directly above the boiling water, in aluminum steaming trays, or in bamboo baskets. The fastest cooking takes place right over the water, as in steaming in a wok that contains a steaming rack. Aluminum steamers cook faster than the bamboo ones; lower stacking trays get more steam pressure (thus requiring fewer minutes) than upper ones.

The following recipes represent approximate steaming times for foods in the bottom tray of an aluminum steamer. Reduce 5 minutes out of 20 if you set the dish on a platform in a wok. Increase 5 minutes for every 20 when you steam in bamboo trays on the bottom or in aluminum racks on top. Add 8 minutes for every 20 for food in the top bamboo trays.

Cooking times are longer when anxious cooks peek inside the steamer — this dissipates the pressure built up there. Go ahead and do it, anyway; an alert cook is an outstanding cook. But allow extra minutes for every look-see.

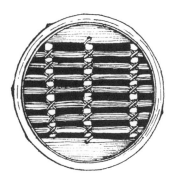

appetizers - memorable morsels

Most Asian meals begin with the main course and end with fresh fruit. Appetizers do exist, however. Dainty dumplings, tasty snacks, and memorable morsels which, prepared beforehand, let the hostess mingle with her guests. Oriental tidbits — especially the meat-filled ones — delicately stave off hunger pangs. I customarily make a small international assortment if dinner is to follow.

Pork and Crab Balls   THAILAND

1 cup sweet rice
1½ cups raw pork
¾ cup cooked crab meat
3 stalks coriander
½ teaspoon ground coriander
1 teaspoon salt
1 teaspoon pepper
1 egg, slightly beaten
2 tablespoons cornstarch
2 cups oil for frying

Preparation: Soak the rice in water for two hours. Drain and set aside. Mince the pork. Set aside. With your hands finely shred the crab meat. Combine with pork. Finely chop the coriander leaves and stalks. Add coriander, ground coriander, salt, pepper, half of the egg, and cornstarch. Mix well. Make 1-inch balls and roll in sweet rice.

Steaming: Line the steamer tray with a wet cotton cloth, set the balls about 1 inch apart, and cook covered 10 minutes. Remove and set aside.

Frying: Heat wok, add oil, and heat oil. Fry several of the steamed balls until the rice becomes golden. Drain on paper towels.

Yield: 3 dozen.

Serving: Insert toothpicks in pork and crab balls for easy nibbling. Make a dip of 2 tablespoons fish sauce, 2 tablespoons white or rice vinegar, and 2 green chili peppers sliced thinly in rings; add a dash of sugar.

Comment: The hot flavor of the chili rings and seeds floating in the dip complements the crunchy sweet rice and tart filling.

Bell Pepper Shrimp Boats   CHINA

3 large bell peppers
¼ pound fresh shrimp
sherry
1 tablespoon cornstarch
10 water chestnuts
1 stalk green onion

Preparation: Halve and seed bell peppers. Slice into 1-inch squares. Arrange on a plate. Set aside. Shell and de-vein shrimp. Marinate in sherry for 15 minutes. Drain and coarsely chop. Place in a small bowl, adding cornstarch. With your fingers, work the cornstarch into the shrimp. Coarsely chop water chestnuts, mince green onion (including the white stalk), and mix with the shrimp. Fill each bell pepper shell with a mound of shrimp and set on a plate.

Cooking: Place dish on platform over boiling water, cover, and steam 10 minutes. Retrieve and serve warm or at room temperature with small dishes of light soy sauce.

Yield: 4 servings.

Possibilities: Use as a *dim sum* serving or as a vegetable. Sprinkle soy sauce and sesame seeds over shrimp. Chopped chillies and fish sauce will give a Vietnamese touch. Bottled chili sauce makes a delicious, tangy dip.

Wasabi Chicken   JAPAN

  2 whole chicken breasts
  ¼ cup white port
  2 teaspoons *wasabi* (Japanese horse radish)
  2½ teaspoons water
  Japanese soy sauce
  ajinomoto (monosodium glutamate)

Preparation: Bone and marinate chicken breasts in wine for four hours. Lay on a plate.

Cooking: Steam covered for 15 minutes. Chill 2 hours. Cut into ½-inch slices. Mix *wasabi* with water. With the end of a chopstick dip the paste and dot each chicken piece. Insert toothpicks for easy serving. Make a dip of 2 tablespoons Japanese soy sauce and four shakes of *ajinomoto*.

Yield: 40 slices.

Shopping tip: Sometimes the meat section of a grocery sells de-boned chicken breasts; these are worth the extra money if you do not plan to use the bones for stock. *Wasabi* is hot; its cool green color can be misleading.

Additional idea: Use steamed chicken (even leftovers) as the main ingredient of a salad. With your fingers shred the breasts into threads about 1-inch long. Slice one cucumber in thin, transparent matchsticks, approximately 2 inches long. Do the same with a carrot. Arrange chicken, cucumber and carrot sticks in small bowls. Toast 1 tablespoon of white sesame seeds and allow to cool. Make a dressing of 3 tablespoons Japanese soy sauce, 2 tablespoons vinegar, and 2 tablespoons of salad oil. Stir in sesame seeds and pour over individual dishes. Serve immediately. Yield: 4 servings.

Three-Meat Dumplings
(Ma Uon)

1 cup raw chicken
1 cup raw pork
¾ cup cooked crab meat
5 stalks coriander
2 green onions
5 cloves garlic
1 teaspoon pepper
1 tablespoon sugar
¼ cup fish sauce
¼ cup coconut cream
¼ cup cornstarch
1 egg, slightly beaten
1 package won ton skins

Preparation: Slice the chicken and pork. Mince together. Finely shred the cooked crab meat. Combine with the chicken and pork mixture. Coarsely chop the coriander leaves, stalks, and roots, the green onions, and the garlic. Mince together and add to meat. Stir in pepper, sugar, fish sauce, coconut cream, cornstarch, and half the egg. Mix well. Set aside.

Wrapping: Cut off the corners of the won ton skins to make circles. Place a teaspoon of the filling in the center of the skin. Gather up the sides, squeezing in the middle to give the dumpling a waist. Flatten top and bottom to shape it like an hourglass.

Cooking: If you use bamboo racks, set dumplings directly on the slats. Aluminum racks need to be lined with a wet cotton cloth to keep them from sticking. Place dumplings on a plate to steam in a wok or electric skillet. Steam, covered, for 15 minutes. Serve warm or at room temperature with or without a dip. To make a dip: combine 2 parts light soy sauce, 1 part sesame oil, and two finely minced green chilies.

Yield: 6 dozen.

Shopping tips: There are varying thicknesses of commercial won ton wrappers. Buy the thinnest ones so the steam will form the dough to the dumpling; thick skins will steam tough and gummy. As a rule, won ton dough in cellophane packages (the kind most supermarkets stock) are thicker and best for deep-frying. I found the thinnest ones wrapped in butcher paper packages on sale in Oriental markets.

Won ton packages bought frozen and then thawed can be frozen again. Of course there is a chance that the cornstarch dusted between every sheet will "melt" into the dough; this makes the pieces stick together. If you are not going to use more than half the package, open it and take out what you need. Freeze the rest before it thaws.

Traditional *Ma Uon* are steamed without dough in tiny ½-inch high cups. Cooked dumplings may be frozen and then reheated in the steamer for 15 minutes.

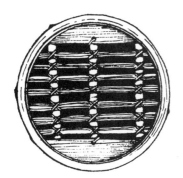

JAPAN
Vinegared Rice Rolled in Seaweed (Norimaki Sushi)

    3 cups short-grain rice
    3 cups water
    ½ cup white vinegar
    ¼ cup *mirin* (sweet rice wine)
    1 tablespoon sugar
    1 teaspoon salt
    8 dried mushrooms
    1 oz. *kanpyo* (dried vegetable gourd strips)
    2 carrots
    8 spinach leaves
    2 eggs, slightly beaten
¼ cup sugar
½ cup soy
¼ cup *mirin*
1 tablespoon vinegar
    10 sheets *nori* (dried seaweed)

Preparation: Rinse rice several times, cover with water, and soak for four hours or overnight. (The water then reaches the core of the grain and cooks it without a hard center.) Drain and add 2 cups water. Bring rice to a boil and cook for 5 minutes or until most of the water has evaporated and the surface of the rice looks moist, Turn heat to low, cover, and steam 10 minutes before removing from the burner to sit 10 minutes. In a small saucepan over low heat dissolve sugar and salt in vinegar and *mirin*. With a wooden paddle criss-cross a pattern of x's deep in the rice to the bottom of the pot, pour in the vinegar mixture, and gently fluff the rice to coat most of the kernels. Set aside. Soak mushrooms for 40 minutes, slice into strips and set aside. Boil carrots 10 minutes, slice into long, thin matchsticks. Set aside. Boil *kanpyo* until strips are translucent, about 40 minutes. Cut into strips the length of the *nori*. Cook eggs into a flat omelette without brown spots; blot on paper towels and cut into long, thin strips. Drop spinach into boiling water for 30 seconds; it'll be limp and bright green. Set aside. Over low heat in a small pan dissolve sugar in soy, *mirin*, and vinegar. Add *kanpyo* strips and carrot strips. Cook 10 minutes, remove, and set aside. Toast seaweed by passing it over a gas flame or electric burner for a few seconds — this dries out the moisture in the sheet.

Rolling: Place the *nori* even with the bottom edge of a *sudare* (a mat of wooden sticks). Scoop ½ cup vinegared rice and spread it with your fingers over two-thirds of the sheet. Wet hands to keep grains from sticking as you pat and distribute the rice in an even layer. Position in the middle of the rice: 3 pieces *kanpyo*, mushroom strips laid tip to tip, spinach in a thin stream, carrots laid tip to tip, and egg strips. Carefully push the *nori* into the rice as you firmly roll the mat. Continue to the end of the seaweed, move the *sushi* to the bottom of the *sudare*, and roll all the way. Pick up the filled mat and squeeze tightly along the cylinder to make the rice stick together. Unroll the mat, place *sushi* seam side down — the moisture from the rice seals the end.

Yield: 10 rolls.

Slicing: Have a clean, sharp knife and a damp cloth nearby. Wet the knife and wipe on the cloth. With a sawing motion, slice the *sushi* into ½-inch pieces. Clean the knife frequently on the cloth whenever the rice sticks to the blade.

Serving: Place cut pieces on a plate, building a pyramid of black disks, each with a different and colorful design in the white rice. Serve chilled or at room temperature. Make a dip of 2 tablespoons Japanese soy sauce and ⅛ teaspoon *ajinomoto* (monosodium glutamate) for each individual saucer.

Custom: *Norimaki Sushi* is one of the favorite types of *sushi*. Originally packed in lacquered, layered boxes for lunch, *sushi* is now accepted as an appetizer and a side dish during dinner. *Sushi* — the vinegared rice — and seafood, fish, and vegetables fill thin egg pancakes and fried bean curd wrappers, too.

Storage, Leftovers, Shopping Tip: *Norimaki sushi* wrapped in wax paper or plastic and refrigerated will keep a day but not overnight; the rice hardens. If you want to make *sushi* another day, keep some of the rice and filling from your initial effort. Rice can be kept unrefrigerated for two days without noticeable loss of quality, but be sure to chill the filling. When you are ready to make *sushi*, put ½ cup of cooked rice for each roll into a small bowl and steam covered for 10 minutes over boiling water. If the vinegar has weakened, add a tablespoon for each *sushi* before steaming.

Black-colored seaweed is superior in taste to green-colored sheets. For small quantities, buy that packaged in cellophane. Machiko Netsu of Austin, Texas purchases *nori* in decorated tins to keep out the Southern humidity. One spring evening Machiko and I made an ample dinner of sushi, fried pork cutlet, and a raw cabbage salad with a vinegar, *ajinomoto*, pepper, soy, and sugar dressing. The sour-sweet taste balanced the crispy meat and the *sushi* provided the rice.

beef, pork & poultry – foods & feasts

BEEF: A LITTLE MAKES A LOT

Beginning Oriental chefs are amazed how far a few thin slices of beef (the thinner the better) will go in preparing a satisfying yet low cholesterol meal. There are economic reasons for this fact. Buddhist religious practices and the scarcity of grazing lands prevent many Asians from using beef, butter, milk, and cheese. Soybean derivatives like fresh bean curd and soybean "milk" replace dairy products and beef as sources of protein in their diets. Consequently, few authentic recipes for Asian beef dishes existed, though several pork recipes can be made with beef instead. If you're using beef as a minced-meat filling for vegetables, don't buy ground beef; it will be tough after cooking. Choose cuts like round, sirloin, or chuck for mincing and slicing. Add a teaspoon of oil for each ½ lb. to insure moistness. When steaming beef by itself, you'll find that slices rather than a minced paste give better results. As with pork patties, you're at liberty to select any topping (and any vegetable) to mix with the meat for a main-dish meal to be served with rice.

Despite the beef shortage, Korean hosts like to offer this meat when guests dine at their home. They barbecue or steam beef short ribs.

Beef Slices with Bamboo Shoots   CHINA
(Jook Soon Jing Gnow Yuke)

> 2 cups beef, sliced
> 1 teaspoon sherry
> 1 tablespoon light soy sauce
> 2 tablespoons oyster sauce
> 1 teaspoon oil
> ½ teaspoon salt
> 1 teaspoon sugar
> 2 teaspoons cornstarch
> ½ cup sliced bamboo shoots

Preparation: Cut beef into ¼-inch slices about 1½ inches long. Place in a deep plate. Add the sherry, light soy sauce, oyster sauce, oil, salt, and sugar. Mix thoroughly. Arrange sliced bamboo shoots over beef.

Cooking: Set plate on a steaming rack, cover, and steam 20 minutes. Stir once to mix the juices before dinner. Serve warm with rice.

Yield: 4 servings.

Slicing tips: Beef slices are tender even when cut from inexpensive chuck and round steaks if the meat is at least 1-inch thick. My mother taught me to divide the meat into 1-inch × 2-inch pieces and then push them on their sides to slice thinly (⅛-¼-inch thick). The idea is to make little steaks out of each chunk. Use slices for steaming and stir-frying. I buy sirloin and tenderloin cuts when I want to make enough for two or three people. If you freeze the beef 15 minutes before slicing, it's easy to make paper-thin steaks.

Minced beef is not as tender as minced pork because beef is leaner. The teaspoon of oil added keeps the beef from drying out before it's cooked. Seasame oil may be substituted for a variation.

Other toppings: Sliced sour bamboo shoots; quartered water chestnuts; broccoli cut in 1-inch pieces; cauliflower cut in 1-inch slices, and carrots in ¼-inch diagonal slices. Blanch broccoli and cauliflower in boiling water one minute and add to beef the last 8 minutes of steaming. Now the beef is a complete meal with rice.

Variation: Omit bamboo shoots for cubes of fresh bean curd. Add 1 tablespoon bean sauce or hot bean sauce. Mix well. Steam 20 minutes.

Beef Short Ribs (Galbi Jim)   KOREA

2 pounds beef short ribs in 3-inch lengths
2 tablespoons sesame seeds
2 green onions
3 cloves garlic
3 slices ginger
2 green chilies
2 teaspoons sesame oil

1 tablespoon dark soy sauce
2 tablespoons brown sugar
1 teaspoon pepper
1 tablespoon sherry
1 tablespoon oil
1 teaspoon cornstarch
2 teaspoons water

Garnish:
shredded green onions

Preparation: Have the butcher saw through the bones to make 3-inch sections. At home, cut into separate ribs. Set aside. In a dry pan, toast sesame seeds, remove, and cool. Pulverize with mortar and pestle or wooden handle of a knife. Set aside. Chop coarsely separately and then combine to mince green onions, garlic, ginger, and chilies. Set aside. In a small bowl, mix sesame oil, soy sauce, brown sugar, pepper, sherry, and sesame seeds. Set aside.

Cooking: Heat oil in a heavy pot, brown green onions, garlic, ginger, and chilies for 2 minutes. Add ribs to brown 3 minutes. Stir in sesame oil mixture, lower heat, cover, and simmer 1 hour. Combine cornstarch and water into a smooth liquid. Before serving, add cornstarch binder and cook 5 minutes longer, stirring constantly. Transfer to a heated platter. Garnish with shredded green onions.

Yield: 4 servings.

Serving suggestions: Steamed bean sprouts and green beans, rice, and *kim chee* (raw vinegared salad) make a home-cooked meal. **Notes:** Everyday brass or wooden chopsticks and China bowls give way to silver utensils on special occasions. Koreans favor beef to pork. Korean seasonings are stronger than Chinese seasonings, with more soy sauce, sesame oil, sesame seeds, garlic, pepper, and chili peppers. Japan, Korea's neighbor to the east, also uses glossy black boxes to serve food. Elaborate carvings of abalone shells on lacquered surfaces decorate Korean furnishings, too.

Beef in Toasted Rice   CHINA

1 cup long-grain rice
1 whole star anise
1 pound flank steak
2 green onions
2 slices ginger
1 tablespoon sherry
2 tablespoons dark soy sauce
1 teaspoon sesame oil

Preparation: In a dry, heavy sauce pan, over high heat, toast star anise and rice to a golden brown — about 5 minutes. Remove. Allow to cool. Place in a blender and grind to crumbs. Set aside. Cut beef into ¾-inch squares and put in a bowl. Shred and mince green onions with ginger. Add to beef, massaging it gently. Pour in sherry, soy sauce, and oil. Marinate for 20 minutes or longer.

Cooking: Coat each piece of flank steak with rice powder and arrange neatly on a plate. Pat extra rice around beef; pour the extra marinade over all. Set plate on a rack over boiling water, cover, steam 1 hour. Retrieve. Serve as the first dish of a dinner.

Yield: 4 servings.

Variation: Substitute brown rice for white and the recipe becomes more nutritious. Steam 1 hour 15 minutes.

Additional idea: Make extra rice powder and store in an air-tight glass jar.

PORK: EVERYDAY FEASTS

The Muslims of Asia don't eat pork, but many Southeast Asians and Chinese eat some pork daily, and the Polynesians feast on a whole pig at festive occasions. Pork is a rich, fatty meat, able to withstand hours of steaming and reheating. Whatever is leftover from lunch — even a few slices — appears on the table again as a side dish for dinner. Chinese meals often feature minced meat patties, usually pork. Hundreds of toppings are possible for these dishes; salted fish is a favorite. The usual Chinese invitation to dinner often includes a mention of *hom yee* — salted fish — in the menu. This fish isn't actually served at parties, however; the expression merely signifies thankfulness that there will be more than salted fish, the ordinary fare of poor people, on the banquet table.

In Fresno, I grew up in a neighborhood of Chinese families who continued their former village life and its types of entertainment in central California. There were always weekly *mah-jong* games, winter and summer; six or eight families would leave the front doors of their houses open, and friends from other parts of town as well as neighbors would casually walk in to visit. Eventually the groups converged on a certain home as the site for the games that particular night. No one made formal preparations, and people often dropped in during our dinner, since (like many Chinese-Americans) we kept grocers' working hours of 9 a.m. to 8 p.m. My Mom and Dad would invite whoever came over to share some of our meal. Curious people just asked outright, "What's cooking?" Mom or Dad would jokingly answer *"hom yee* and minced pork patty," laughing; our table displayed winter melon soup, lobster in black bean sauce, steamed hearts of *bok choy*, and stir-fried chicken with yard beans, so the visitor knew full well he would hardly be served such simple fare.

Spicy Pork Coins   THAILAND

1⅓ cups raw pork
4 cloves garlic
1 teaspoon ground coriander
8 teaspoons light soy sauce
2 teaspoons black pepper
1 teaspoon sugar
2 cups oil

Preparation: Mince pork. Set aside. Mince garlic and combine with pork. Add ground coriander, soy sauce, pepper, and sugar. Mix well. Make 1-inch balls and flatten into thick coins.

Cooking: Line a steamer rack with a wet cotton cloth. Bring water to boil, lay pieces on cloth, cover, and steam 10 minutes. With chopsticks, tongs, or a spoon, retrieve pork disks from the cloth before it dries. Pour oil into a heated wok, heat the oil, and

fry several patties until golden and crispy, about 1 minute. Drain on paper towels. Serve warm with a dip of 2 tablespoons fish sauce, 2 tablespoons white vinegar, and 2 minced green chilies.

Yield: 1½ dozen.

Possibilities: Can be a side dish or an appetizer. Sometimes I only make 5 meat patties for a side dish and use a tablespoon of oil in a small saucepan to fry them. Transfer the steamed patties from the steamer directly to the hot oil and you won't need to use an extra plate. This recipe has the Thai flavors of lots of garlic, pepper, coriander, fish sauce and chilies.

Steamed Minced Pork   CHINA
(Jing Gee Yuke)

2 cups raw pork
⅓ cup water chestnuts
1 tablespoon light soy sauce
2 teaspoons dark soy sauce
½ teaspoon sugar
2 teaspoons cornstarch

Preparation: Mince pork. Set aside. Finely chop water chestnuts (save a tablespoon for garnish) and combine with pork. Add light soy sauce, dark soy sauce, sugar, and cornstarch. Mix well. Pat lightly into a deep dish. Sprinkle minced water chestnut over pork patty.

Cooking: Bring water to a boil, set plate on rack, and steam 30 minutes. Serve warm with rice.

Yield: 4 servings.

Comments: Steamed minced pork dishes are the

mainstays of Chinese home-cooked meals. Variations include: bamboo shoots, preserved Szechwan cabbage (*jar choy*), fresh and dried mushrooms, or Chinese preserved turnips in place of water chestnuts. Salted fish, tea melon, bean curd (*tofu*) or Chinese sausage (*lop cheong*) top the pork while it's steaming.

Cooking and shopping tips: A small piece of fat minced in with the pork gives it a smoother texture. A teaspoon of oil will help if the meat is especially lean. You may buy a large pork butt or tenderloin and freeze portions of it for later use. I prefer to buy an assorted selection of loin cuts — I use two chops to make a side dish of minced pork, and then freeze the bones for chicken broth which transforms canned soup into a rich, homemade stock.

Minced pork may be reheated 15 minutes two or three times depending on how much fat is in the dish. Small amounts placed on top of a rice pot to reheat also flavor the rice.

CHINA

Spareribs in Black Bean Sauce (Dow See Jing Pie Quat)

  2 pounds pork spareribs in 2-inch pieces
  2 cloves garlic
  1 slice ginger
  2 tablespoons *dow see* (fermented salted black beans)
  ¼ cup dark soy sauce
  2 tablespoons sherry
  ¼ cup water

Preparation: Have the butcher cut the sparerib bones into 2-inch lengths. Separate into individual pieces. Parboil ribs for 20 minutes, drain, and set aside. Rinse the black beans in water. Mince the garlic, shred the ginger. Mash the garlic with the black beans. Sprinkle black bean mixture and ginger strips over the spareribs. Add the dark soy sauce and sherry.

Cooking: Place plate on steaming rack. Cover and steam 30 minutes to 2 hours. Remove. Heat an empty wok, add ribs, brown for 30 seconds. Pour in sauce, add water, and continue browning for 90 seconds. Return ribs with sauce to the steamer plate to warm until dinner is ready. Stir the spareribs in the sauce before serving.

Yield: 4 servings.

Serving suggestion: Can be steamed with a fish at the same time to make a meal for four people.

Shopping tips: In buying ribs, look for at least an even distribution of fat and meat over the bone, with more meat if possible. This dish can be reheated 30 minutes in the steamer or a saucepan without changing its taste. (In fact, it improves since the pork becomes more tender with more steaming as the fat breaks down.) Add ½ - 1 cup water for more sauce the second time. Salted black beans is a Cantonese seasoning for steamed fish and seafood and stir-fried meats. Be warned: guests invariably ask for this recipe.

Kalua Pork   HAWAII

  4 pounds pork butt, loin, or shoulder roast
  salt
  ti and banana leaves
  string

Preparation: Remove excess fat from pork. Slice

into 1-inch thick pieces. Lightly salt and squeeze meat to make it firm. Set aside. Rinse *ti* and banana leaves. Wipe water off with your hand. The *ti* leaves wrap the pork; the banana leaves cover the *ti* leaves. Cut off stems of *ti* leaves so they will fold. Lay meat at narrower end of *ti* leaf and roll to its end. Now enclose the *ti* leaf parcel in the banana leaf the same way. Secure with string.

Cooking: Bring eight inches of water to boil in the steamer pot, build a pyramid of flat packages on one tray, cover, and steam 4 hours. After 2 hours, shift the top pork parcels to the bottom.

Serving: Remove packages and serve hot.

Yield: 6 servings.

Custom: A whole *Kalua* pig cooks 5-6 hours in a pit with fire-heated rocks at the bottom; a grid of wooden stakes lies on the rocks, covered with banana and palm fronds. Tender, succulent pork inevitably results from this traditional accompaniment for happy events.

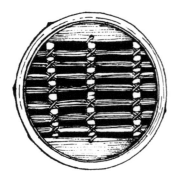

POULTRY: STAPLE OF ASIA

Fowl — especially chicken — plays an important part in the food of Asians. Its role in Oriental meals is as major as the traditional place of beef in North Americans' diet. As one walks through American Chinatowns, live ducks and chickens squawk in their sidewalk cages, waiting to be bought. Roasted ducks dangle from hooks in the butcher-shop windows. Deep-fried squabs are a favorite delicacy for special occasions in Chinatown restaurants. Steamed chicken is everyday fare for Chinese (except when served cold) but its succulence is never taken for granted. Chickens are expensive in India and are considered party food; in Polynesia, too, cooks reserve chickens for parties. People in Hong Kong keep them caged in their apartments near the kitchen.

Fried, deep-fried, roasted, boiled, braised, or steamed — poultry continues to be a staple of Asian menus.

Red Date Chicken　　　CHINA

    8 chicken thighs
    12 lily flowers
    4 dried mushrooms
    6 red dates
    2 pieces ginger
    1 tablespoon dark soy sauce
    ½ teaspoon salt
    ½ teaspoon pepper
    ½ teaspoon sugar
    1 teaspoon sesame oil
    2 tablespoons sherry
    2 teaspoons cornstarch
    1 Chinese sausage (optional)

Preparation: Remove skin of chicken thighs. Put meat in a deep plate. Soak lily flowers, dried mushrooms, and red dates in water for 30 minutes or until they are soft. Knot the flowers and cut off the tough ends. Slice mushrooms into thin pieces. Halve the red dates to remove the seed. Sliver ginger. Sprinkle all over chicken. Add dark soy, salt, pepper, sugar, sesame oil, and sherry. Mix cornstarch well with chicken and other ingredients. Pat neatly in dish. Slice sausage in diagonal cuts and arrange on top of chicken.

Cooking: Set plate over boiling water in covered steamer for 30 minutes. Stir once before serving warm with rice.

Yield: 4 servings.

Notes: Dark meat (with its higher fat content) is preferable for steaming; white meat is usually best in quick stir-fried recipes. You can steam chicken thighs up to an hour and they stay tender while other dishes steam below them. Transfer the Red Date Chicken to the top tray to keep warm. People who normally avoid the dark meat of chicken like this kind of juicy chicken.

Variation: White meat becomes tough if you steam it again; it is delicious one time only. Bone 3 whole chicken breasts; remove skin. Slice into 1-inch pieces, mix with other ingredients, and steam 10 minutes. Stir once to baste chicken. Seldom served in restaurants, this is a favorite home-cooked meal for Chinese. Small amounts can be reheated if you lay the parts over a pot of cooked rice after its boil for the last 20 minutes of steaming and resting.

Pressed Almond Duck　　CHINA
with Peach Sauce
(Wo Siu Op)

    1 5-pound frozen duck
    water
    3 pieces of ginger, the size of quarters
    1 clove garlic
    ⅓ cup dark soy sauce
    ¼ cup sherry
    3 pieces star anise
    1 tablespoon sugar
    salt
    ½ cup water chestnut powder
    oil for deep-frying
    2 tablespoons crushed almonds
    1 stalk green onion, shredded

Peach sauce:
    ⅓ cup brown sugar
    ¾ cup water
    ⅓ cup vinegar
    2 tablespoons catsup
    2 tablespoons cornstarch
    2 fresh peaches

Preparation: Thaw duck to room temperature, about 10 hours or overnight. Rinse and dry with paper towels.

Cooking: Crush ginger and garlic. Put duck in a large pot, fill with water, add ginger, garlic, soy, sherry, star anise, and sugar. Bring to a boil for 3 minutes and lower heat to medium for 1 hour. Turn off heat, wait 20 minutes, remove duck. Bone duck, finely shred the meat into 1-inch lengths with your fingers, cut up the skin into 2-inch squares. Arrange half of the meat in a square 7-inch pan and sprinkle with salt. Press 2 tablespoons water chestnut powder on the meat. Arrange the other half of the meat on top of the first layer, sprinkle with salt, and press 2 tablespoons water chestnut powder onto this meat. Cover duck with squares of skin, press firmly, sprinkle with salt, and pat more water chestnut powder on this to make a ½-inch thickness.

Steaming and Frying: Place pan on steamer rack and steam 20 minutes. Remove and let cool. (You can refrigerate it overnight.) Cut the duck patty into 1½-inch squares. Coat with water chestnut powder. Heat 2 cups of oil in a wok or deep fryer and fry pieces until brown, about 1 minute. Drain on paper towels.

Serving: Arrange squares on a platter, building three-story pyramids. Cover with peach sauce, crushed almonds, and shredded green onion. To make peach sauce: dice peaches. Stir together sugar, water, vinegar, catsup, and peaches in a small saucepan. Cook until sauce thickens, stirring constantly. Place contents in a blender and whip for 2 seconds. Pour over pressed duck.

Cooking hints: Freeze fresh peach sauce in a glass jar in the summer months and enjoy it during the winter. Thaw and reheat. If sauce is too tart because of sour-tasting peaches, sweeten with 2 tablespoons brown sugar. Control the thickness of the sauce with more or less cornstarch. When adding extra thickening, mix 1 tablespoon cornstarch with 2 tablespoons water and slowly pour into the rest of

the sauce. Cook the sauce 5 minutes longer. Use kitchen shears to cut duck skin into squares and to shred the meat finer.

Serving suggestion: This exquisitely juicy duck steals the show every time. Delicious with shredded lettuce and with a chicken salad. Or place fried duck pieces on a bed of shredded lettuce and pour sauce over all. The soft texture of steamed flounder nicely balances the crunchy quality of pressed duck.

Yield: 4 servings.

Garlic Chicken (Dak Jim) KOREA

1 3-pound chicken
2 tablespoons white sesame seeds
4 cloves garlic
4 green onions
⅓ cup light soy sauce
1 teaspoon chili powder
½ teaspoon black pepper
2 tablespoons sesame oil

Preparation: Wash and dry chicken. Cut breasts in six pieces; disjoint drumstick, thighs, and wings. (The back may be left whole since it doesn't have much meat — bone it later to save for a chicken salad.) Set all in a heavy pot. In a dry, hot pan toast sesame seeds to a golden color. Remove, allow to cool, and set aside for a garnish. Coarsely chop garlic and green onions and mince together. Combine with chicken. Add soy sauce, chili powder, black pepper, and sesame oil. Mix well with a wooden spoon. Marinate at room temperature 2 hours or overnight in the refrigerator.

Cooking: Turn burner setting to low and cook chicken 1 hour, stirring occasionally. The liquid increases in the pot as the chicken cooks. Transfer chicken pieces to a serving platter, pour some of the sauce over them, and sprinkle sesame seeds over all. Serve with white rice, *kim chee* salad (pickled cabbage) and raw spinach as the vegetable.

Yield: 4 servings.

Additional idea: Well-scrubbed radishes dipped in sesame oil and served as the vegetable complement the tender chicken.

Comments: Steamed meats like *Dak Jim* are notable exceptions to the usual Korean diet of blanched vegetables, barbecued meats, and boiled white short-grain rice. This method of steam-cooking is similar to the Indian style of cooking with a little liquid over low fire.

Whole Steamed Chicken ASIA

1 3-pound chicken
2 tablespoons salad oil
½ teaspoon salt

Preparation: Wash chicken, pat dry with paper towels, place in a plate with at least a 2-inch rim.

Steaming: Bring 6 inches of water to boil in the steamer pot. (It heats faster in a covered pot.) Set dish on tray, cover, steam 50 minutes. While chicken is cooking, heat salad oil and allow to cool. Retrieve chicken out of plate (discard fat or use to flavor vegetables), allow to cool 10 minutes, brush oil over chicken, then salt. Bone chicken with skin, arrange pieces in a decorated platter.

Yield: 4 servings.

Serving: Serve warm, at room temperature, or

chilled. Vary the recipe with ginger, sesame, soy, or canned plum sauces. Garnish with toasted sesame seeds, shredded green onions, or chili flowers.

Reheating: Since the chicken is not over-cooked, cover and reheat 10 minutes over boiling water. Garnish and serve.

Idea for Entertaining: This is an excellent recipe to double or triple beforehand and chill. On every plate of chicken, add a different sauce and garnish before serving for a buffet.

Ginger Chicken   MALAYSIA

    1 whole steamed chicken
    1 tablespoon oil
    2 tablespoons minced ginger
    3 minced green chilies
    ½ teaspoon sugar
    1 teaspoon sesame oil

Garnish:
    green onion fronds, p. 51.

Preparation: Bone steamed chicken and arrange neatly in a deep plate. Set aside.

Make sauce: Heat a small saucepan with oil, brown ginger and green chilies for 1 minute, stir in sugar and sesame oil. Cook to dissolve sugar. Turn off heat.

Serving: Pour sauce over chicken. Garnish with green onions. Serve warm or at room temperature.

Yield: 4 servings.

Storage: If you plan to serve it later, cover the chicken and refrigerate. Later allow the chicken to come to room temperature, pour heated sauce over it, and garnish.

THAILAND

Chicken with Nam Prik Gapi

    1 cucumber
    ½ head iceberg lettuce
    1 steamed chicken
    2 cloves garlic
    1 green chili
    2 teaspoons shrimp paste
    juice of 1 lime
    1 teaspoon sugar
    1 teaspoon fish sauce

Preparation: Slice cucumber into ¼-inch pieces, shred lettuce, and arrange on a decorated platter. Set aside. Bone steamed chicken and place parts over lettuce. Set aside.

To make nam prik gapi: Mince garlic and green chili. Place in mortar and crush with pestle. (If you don't have these utensils, mince the garlic and chili as fine as possible.) Put in a small bowl. Add shrimp paste (from plastic jar) and mash well. Stir in lime juice. Add sugar and fish sauce and dissolve sugar by stirring. Transfer to small individual dishes for dipping. Or you can simply pour the sauce over the chicken.

Yield: 4 servings.

Storage: Refrigerate *nam prik gapi* in a covered glass jar up to a month. Serve at room temperature.

Boneless Sesame Chicken   CHINA

1 whole steamed chicken
2 teaspoons sesame oil
1 tablespoon minced ginger
2 teaspoons light soy sauce
1 tablespoon *teriyaki* sauce
½ teaspoon sugar

Garnish:
toasted sesame seeds
finely shredded green onions

Preparation: Bone a steamed chicken, arrange over a bed of lettuce or plain plate, then set aside. Heat sesame oil in a small saucepan, brown the ginger, add soy sauce, *teriyaki* sauce, and sugar. Stir to dissolve sugar.

Serving: Pour sauce over chicken, sprinkle sesame seeds and scatter green onions. Serve warm or at room temperature.

Yield: 4 servings.

Leftovers: Refrigerate and reheat 10 minutes or eat chilled. It's delicious either way.

MALAYSIA

Aromatic Chicken with Rice

3 cups cooked rice
1 3-pound chicken
1 onion
3 tablespoons sesame oil
2 tablespoons light soy sauce
½ teaspoon salt
¼ teaspoon pepper

Preparation: Spread cooked rice in a pie pan. Set

aside. Chop chicken into large pieces. Cut onion in wedges. In a wok, heat sesame oil, brown chicken and onion until onion is transparent. Add soy sauce, sprinkle with salt and pepper. Transfer chicken to rice; pour sauce over chicken and rice.

Cooking: Set dish on rack over boiling water, cover, and steam 30 minutes or until the chicken is done. Sprinkle with bottled chili sauce. Serve warm with steamed vegetables.

Yield: 4 servings.

Alternative steamer: If you own a rice cooker, place braised chicken in the water with the raw rice. Cook until rice is steamed.

VIETNAM

Chicken with Chopped Tomatoes

1 3-pound chicken
4 slices ginger
1 tablespoon sesame oil
2 tablespoons fish sauce
½ teaspoon pepper

Garnish:
1 tomato
1 stalk green onion

Chili Sauce:
2 red chilies
2 cloves garlic
2 tablespoons fish sauce
½ teaspoon sugar
1 tablespoon vinegar
1 tablespoon lemon juice

Preparation: Chop chicken into large pieces, arrange in a deep dish, set aside. Slice ginger into matchsticks, scatter over chicken. Mix in sesame oil, fish sauce, and pepper.

Cooking: Bring a pot of water to boil in steamer pot, place dish on rack, cover, and steam 25-30 minutes (over-cooking toughens fowl). While dish is cooking, chop tomato (at room temperature) and green onions. Set aside. Make chili sauce: finely mince chilies and garlic, transfer to a small bowl. Mash with the heel of a knife or cleaver. Stir in sugar until it dissolves. Add fish sauce, vinegar, and lemon juice.

Serving: Retrieve dish, transfer chicken to heated plate, garnish with chopped tomato and green onions. Serve warm with rice and hot and spicy chili sauce as a dip.

Yield: 4 servings.

Chicken and Butterfish in Ti Leaves (Laulau)   HAWAII

1 pound butterfish
½ pound raw chicken breasts
½ pound lean pork
1 teaspoon salt
20 *ti* leaves
10 taro leaves

Preparation: Slice fish into 10 pieces. Set aside. Bone chicken breasts and dice into ½-inch pieces. Set aside. Dice pork into ¼-inch bits. Set aside. Heat a wok with 2 tablespoons oil and stir-fry pork 2 minutes, add chicken and cook 1 minute longer. Season with salt. Remove.

Preparing ti leaves: Take 10 leaves and cut off stems (these will be the interior leaves). Lay aside. With a small sharp knife cut part of the stem from the underside of the remaining leaves and peel away to the center of each leaf (save rib for tying). Set aside. Rinse and dry taro leaves.

Wrapping: Place fish in center of taro leaf, scoop ½ cup of stir-fried pork and chicken over fish, and overlap leaf ends. Set aside with seam side down. Repeat until all taro leaves are folded. Now position two *ti* leaves at a cross — exterior leaf underside up, interior leaf shiny side up. Set the taro leaf package off center toward the tip of the interior leaf. Pick up the tip and roll over taro leaf bundle, then continue to roll to the end of the leaf. Return parcel to bottom third of the exterior leaf, its open ends facing the tip and stem. Fold the tip over the interior leaf and continue almost to the end of the leaf. With the sharp point of a knife, slit an opening to tuck in the stem. Tie with the saved rib or string around the open ends of the leaf. Repeat until all *ti* leaves are used.

Steaming: Bring 6 inches of water to boil in the steamer pot, place *ti*-leaf envelopes about 1 inch apart directly on the trays. Cover and steam 30 minutes.

Yield: 10 servings.

Serving: Bring steaming trays to tables where guests can choose their parcels. Have a large empty bowl nearby to collect the leaves. Steamed bananas and yams, a *Kalua* pig, *poi* (pounded taro roots), and salted salmon fill out a banquet menu.

Custom: *Laulaus* are always served at *luaus* — the Hawaiian feasts for happy occasions. People generally eat on straw mats surrounded by greenery — tropical plants, orchids and plumeria flowers, banana-leaf plates, coconut cups, scooped out watermelons filled with fresh fruit — listening to the

steel guitars of Hawaiian music. Hawaiian men (like the Japanese men who generally cook for special events) put *laulaus* in the underground oven to steam with the pig.

Shopping tips: Purchase *bok choy* or swiss chard for the leaves if taro leaves are not available. In a pinch, buy spinach leaves. Banana leaves substitute for *ti* leaves, although the latter can be ordered from florists in San Francisco.

Variation: Chop taro leaves and cook with chicken and pork. Use four *ti* leaves instead of two. Cut stems off all leaves. Lay leaves across each other to close any space where filling might leak. Place fish (mullet or flounder) in center and cover with 1 cup filling. Gather the leaves and twist to form bags. Tie with string. Set on trays over boiling water, cover, and steam 40 minutes. No unwrapping needed — at the table un-twist the leaves and eat with your fingers, Polynesian style!

Chicken Rice (Tori Meshi)   JAPAN

    2 cups rice
    2 cups chicken broth to use for rice and *gu*

Gu mixture:
    ¼ cup dried mushrooms
    ½ cup raw chicken
    ¼ cup bamboo shoots
    ½ *konnyaku* (yam noodle cake)
    1 carrot
    ¼ *kamaboko* (steamed fish cake)

Gu seasoning:
    ¼ cup mushroom liquid
    2 tablespoons *saké* (rice wine)
    2 tablespoons chicken stock

2 teaspoons sugar
½ teaspoon salt
2 tablespoons Japanese soy sauce

Rice seasoning:
1 tablespoon *saké*
1 tablespoon sugar
¾ teaspoon salt
¼ cup Japanese soy sauce

Preparation: Soak rice in water four hours or longer. Set aside.

To Make Gu: Soak mushrooms in water 20 minutes, squeeze dry (save liquid), and slice into ¼-inch pieces. Also cut (in the same size): raw chicken, bamboo shoots, *konnyaku*, carrot, and *kamaboko*. Combine in a small bowl the mushroom juice, *saké*, and chicken stock, and set aside. In a saucepan, heat 1 tablespoon oil, and partially cook chicken. Stir in *konnyaku*, bamboo shoots, and carrots. Cook 2 minutes. Add contents of small bowl. Drop in mushrooms and cook 2 minutes. Now season with sugar, salt, and soy sauce. Add *kamaboko* strips and cook until sugar dissolves. Set aside.

To make rice: Drain rice. Set aside. Measure 1½ cups stock into a large pot, bring to a boil, and add rice seasonings of *saké*, sugar, salt, and soy sauce. Stir rice into stock and cook as for boiled rice, p. 63. Put the cooked *gu* over the rice when you cover the pot. When ready to serve, add steamed snow peas or parboiled frozen peas. Gently mix to distribute the *gu* evenly with the rice. Serve hot.

Yield: 4 servings.

Reheating: Make ahead of time, refrigerate, then cover and reheat in a deep dish over boiling water for 20 minutes.

Chicken in Yogurt (Dahi Murgh)   INDIA

1 2½-3 pound chicken
1 carton unflavored yogurt
2 tablespoons oil
1 medium onion, chopped
1 tablespoon minced ginger
1 teaspoon minced garlic
2 teaspoons minced green chilies
3 tablespoons fresh lemon juice

Preparation: Chop chicken into large pieces: wings, thighs, drumsticks, breasts, back.

Cooking: Place yogurt in a deep pot, put chicken in, turn heat to low, cover, and cook 50 minutes. While chicken is cooking, heat oil in a saucepan, and brown the onion until transparent. Add ginger, garlic, and green chilies and fry 5 minutes. Pour over chicken, cover, and continue cooking.

Serving: Before serving, stir in lemon juice. An incredibly tasty dish emerges from these simple steps.

Yield: 4 servings.

Extra servings: The steamer pot accommodates two chickens if you double the recipe.

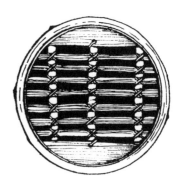

steaming the sea—
reaping the waves

Most of Asia fronts on seas; streams and rivers run throughout every country. Japan, the Philippines, Indonesia, Malaysia, Hawaii, and Tahiti are part or all oceanic islands. India, Burma, Thailand, Vietnam, China, and Korea have coastlines that touch the Sea of Japan, the China Seas, the Bay of Bengal, and other seas. Monsoons inundate the interior waterways once a year to deliver a rice crop at the end of the three-month wet season, and after these daily rains the fish feed voraciously. Taking advantage of this occurrence, the people throw their lines from sampans and wade in the water with spears and nets. They constantly hunt the larger fish with ships.

While Asia does not have the acreage to graze cattle, it has the water environment for mullet, butterfish, pomfret, squirrel fish, tuna, catfish, mudfish, mahi-mahi, and carp. The varieties differ from those found in North America, though some names are similar. Asians prefer firm white fishes such as sea bass and cod, but they cannot resist steaming delicate trout and the soft carp, as well. Wherever the coconut palm and the banana tree grow, natives wrap seafood and fish in leaves. Crab and clam shells function as impromptu steaming racks everywhere.

A white fish such as flounder or whiting — strewn with strips of bamboo shoots, black mushrooms, carrots, and garnished with green onions — can convert the skeptic who thinks of steamed food as drab and tasteless. The traditional method is to serve a fresh fish complete with its head and tail, but steaks and fillets are just as flavorsome and sometimes more convenient, especially when there's only one or two people. Commercially frozen fish generally disappoints the cook.

A one-and-a-half-pound fish is the equivalent of one pound of fillets or steaks. Steam covered 15 to 20 minutes (whole) or 10 to 15 minutes (fillets and steaks). The whole fish is cooked when its eyes turn milky white and a sizeable amount of liquid has seeped out of the flesh. When a fillet looks white and feels firm, it's done. Fish should not be mushy. If it is, it's underdone; put it back to cook longer until flaky. If it feels coarse, it's overdone. A thick fish takes more time to steam than a thin one. I have steamed fillets of sole in five minutes, surprising guests with their thoroughly cooked texture. A few practices will train your eye for the right look. Figure a pound or less for two people's main dish and four diners' side dish. Add 10 minutes for steaming two fishes laid side by side.

Fish is the most improtant source of protein in Asia and is therefore treated with respect. To reach the flesh on the bottom side of the bone, do not overturn the fish (this is a bad omen for ships at sea; you might cause some vessel to sink, according to a Cantonese superstition). Instead, remove the bone by lifting it out ceremonially.

Most guests will be interested in knowing the species of fish they are enjoying; this fact is important to Asians. My Grandmother Wong knew all the names of fishes near the Si River in southeast China. When she first came to the United States she would not eat a fish until she knew its precise name. My frustrated father asked more questions of the fish market owner in one month than he ever had in 30 years. Your friends and family will soon learn the noticeable differences between steamed redfish and trout, sea bass and whiting.

Any fish can be steamed with any sauce, but I shall name the classic ways to serve it together with

31

variations in parenthesis. Begin with Crispy Onion Fish or Kwantung Fish and try all the sauces. Just keep your eye on the timer and replenish the water if you need to. And try not to feel guilty about doing so little work for the spectacular and delicious results of steaming a fish.

KWANTUNG PROVINCE

Kwantung Fish   CHINA
(Jing Yue)

1 2-pound fresh sea bass with head and tail
1 teaspoon salt
2 slices ginger
1 green onion
⅓ cup oil
⅓ cup light soy sauce

Preparation: Wash, scale, and remove entrails from fish if the fish man did not do it. Dry and place in a deep plate. Salt the fish. Slash with a knife in two places on both sides. Shred ginger and green onion. Set aside.

Cooking: Make sure the water is boiling before you put the fish in to cook so you can time from that point. Set plate on rack, cover, and steam 20 minutes. Before the fish is ready, heat the oil *HOT*. Take the plate out of the steamer, pour off liquid in plate, scatter the shredded ginger and green onion over the fish. Drizzle the soy, then the oil, on the puffing fish (the sizzle always brings people into the kitchen). Serve immediately.

Yield: 4 servings.

Leftovers: The flavors are subtle yet distinct. Guests will be picking at the bones even when the fish is finished. Should you have some left over, eat it the next day cold or at room temperature. However, a one-inch thick fish in a sauce reheated 15 minutes is still delicious. Another cooking dries out the fish and its texture coarsens.

Serving suggestion: While the fish is steaming, make a stir-fried beef dish and serve both at the same time with warm rice.

Variation: Slice a 1-inch chunk of ginger into thin strips. Brown in oil to crispy curls. Distribute over fish after oil has been poured. This adds a hot taste to the sauce.

Spicy Fish   INDIA
(Patra Ni Machi)

2 pounds thick (¾-inch) cod steaks
salt
2 small onions
3 slices ginger
2 cloves garlic
2 green chilies
8 stalks fresh coriander
1 lemon
1 teaspoon ground cumin
1 cup fresh coconut crumbs
2 tablespoons *ghee* (clarified butter)
banana leaves
1 teaspoon *garam masala* (powdered seasoning)

Preparation: Lightly salt fish steaks on both sides. Set aside. Chop one onion, place in blender. Slice ginger, garlic, green chilies, and coriander. Put in blender. Peel and seed lemon. Chop coarsely, add to onion mixture in blender. Whip 30 seconds, scraping down sides if necessary. Blend another 10 seconds. Add fresh coconut. Blend 5 seconds. Set aside. Chop second onion. In a small plan, heat *ghee*, add onion and brown until transparent, pour in mixture from blender. Cook 2 minutes, stirring constantly. Turn off heat, add *garam masala*. Allow to cool.

Wrapping: Wash banana leaves in water, wipe off excess with your hand, and cut into pieces 2 inches wider than the length of steak. Pat some coconut-onion mixture firmly on each side of the fish. Lay crossways on banana leaf. Fold edges over fish, then roll the fish to the end of the leaf. Fasten with a thin toothpick or tie with string. Place one inch apart on steamer rack over boiling water. Cover and steam for 30 minutes. (If you are not using a steamer, place parcels on plate and then on a trivet.) Retrieve.

Yield: 4 servings.

Serving suggestions: Serve warm or at room temperature with one or two vegetables, rice, and a *raitha* (a salad of yogurt and vegetables — either cucumbers or onion and tomatoes). Iced water or beer perks up the meal, whereas heavy-tasting liquor masks the flavor of the spices.

Shopping tips: *Garam masala* is a seasoning borrowing the spices from curry-making. Add *garam masala* at the end; it is not cooked like curry. Purchase the spice in bottles from the Oriental markets or make your own brand. In India, the curry spice and the *garam masala* are made before every meal. Cinnamon sticks, peppercorns, whole seeds of coriander, cumin, mustard, cardamon, whole cloves and fenugreek are roasted individually and then ground separately with mortar and pestle before being mixed into special blends. Ground spices can be used; when kept in a can, they stay potent for months. Here is a sample of *garam masala* that will fill a small glass bottle: 4

teaspoons ground coriander, 2 teaspoons ground cumin, 1½ teaspoons ground pepper, 1 teaspoon ground cardamon, 2 teaspoons ground cinnamon, and ½ teaspoon ground cloves. If you can identify the spice you favor, add more of that spice next time.

To clarify butter (that is, to remove the milk solids), melt butter in a saucepan until the white solids sink to the bottom and the surface looks clouded. Skim off this froth, pour butter (except for solids) into a bowl. Allow to cool and then chill. Skim more froth off and scrape the pure translucent yellow butterfat into another pan, leaving more solids in the bowl. Heat the fat again and strain through a cheesecloth to rid it of all milk solids. Now the *ghee* keeps without refrigeration, doesn't burn like butter, and adds the special flavor (like *fresh* coconut does) to Indian recipes. Yogurt and *ghee* characterize many north Indian dishes. Originally *ghee* meant clarified buffalo butter, not cow butter, since the cow and its products were considered sacred and not for humans.

VIETNAM
Cellophane-Noodle Fish (Cá Hấp)

1 1½-2 pound red snapper with head and tail
salt
one 2-ounce package cellophane noodles
(dried mung bean noodles)
6 dried mushrooms
1 carrot
4 slices ginger
2 cloves garlic
2 tablespoons fish sauce
2 tablespoons light soy sauce
¼ teaspoon salt

½ teaspoon pepper
1 stalk coriander
1 green onion
3 medium-sized tomatoes

Preparation: Wash, scale, and dry fish. Lightly salt. Score fish in several places on both sides. Place in a plate with a ½-inch rim. Soak noodles and mushrooms in the same bowl of water until soft, about 25 minutes. Remove mushrooms, stem, and slice into ¼-inch pieces. Set aside. Cut carrots into matchsticks. Set aside. Sliver ginger and garlic. Set aside. In a small bowl, mix fish sauce, light soy sauce, salt, and pepper. Stir in noodles, mushrooms, carrots, ginger, and garlic. Chop coriander coarsely. Cut green onions in 2-inch lengths. Slice tomatoes in thick wedges. Pour fish sauce combination over fish, scatter coriander and green onions over all. Decorate with tomato wedges at the sides.

Cooking: Place dish on steamer rack over boiling water, cover, and steam 30 minutes. Serve warm with bowls of white rice and chopsticks.

Yield: 4 servings.

Variation: Rinse two tablespoons of fermented salted black beans and mix with fish sauce mixture before steaming.

Leftovers: This receipe reheats well, probably on account of its sauce and the thickness of the red snapper. Place in covered pan for 20 minutes.

Comment: Many Vietnamese are bilingual in the Chinese and Vietnamese languages, and the mutual influence extends further than language. Chinese immigrants have lived in Vietnam for centuries and have merged native seasonings — fish sauce, coriander — with Chinese methods of cooking and eating. Vietnam uses chopsticks, for instance, the

only country in Southeast Asia that does. This recipe depends on fish sauce, whose use is as common in Vietnam as soysauce in China and Japan.

CAMBODIA

Fish in Banana Leaves (Pa Khing)

1 1½-2 pound fish steak (rockfish is nice)
salt
5 slices ginger
4 cloves garlic
1 lemon
2 tablespoons sesame seeds
2 tablespoons sesame oil
banana leaves
toothpicks

Preparation: Wash and dry steaks, if necessary. Lightly salt. Set aside. Slice ginger in threads. Sliver garlic. Cut lemon crosswise into thin circles. Set aside. In a dry pan over high heat, toast sesame seeds to a dark brown. Remove. Add sesame oil to pan and brown garlic to a golden color. Remove from heat, stir in sesame seeds. While sesame mixture is cooling, rinse banana leaves with water and wipe off excess with your hand. Cut leaves into long strips, place fish steaks at the end of the leaf, pour sesame seed mixture over it, sprinkle with ginger strips, and garnish with lemon slices. Carefully roll the leaf to its end and secure the open sides with thin toothpicks.

Steaming: Place wrapped packages directly on the steamer racks over boiling water, cover, and steam for 20 minutes. (If steamer isn't used, lay fish on plate, then on steaming rack. Steam 15 minutes.)

Yield: 4 servings.

Serving: Each guest gets a parcel which they unwrap at the table. Have a large bowl nearby to discard the leaves. At times, I set the entire steaming basket on the table as a decorative serving platter. Guests then choose their slices of fish steak.

Shopping hint: Banana leaves bought frozen from the Oriental markets are best when the leaves are green and show no yellow edges. One should be careful about using a banana leaf that grows in someone's yard down the block; chemicals sprayed on the leaf cannot be removed. Those tree leaves were meant to be decorative. If the purchased leaves are split, cover the fish with a few pieces and wrap in aluminum foil. The scent of the banana leaves transfers to the fish, whereas aluminum foil adds no flavor.

THAILAND
Fish with Hot Bean Sauce

    2 pounds fish steaks (bass, halibut)
    1-inch chunk of ginger
    4 cloves garlic
    1 stalk celery
    2 green chilies
    1 small onion
    2 tablespoons oil
    2 tablespoons hot bean sauce
    1 cup water
    1 teaspoon sugar
    1 tablespoon fish sauce
    2 teaspoons cornstarch
    1 tablespoon water
    1 teaspoon vinegar

Garnish:
    2 green onions
    ¼ head iceberg lettuce.

Preparation and Steaming: Rinse fish steaks; lightly salt, and set in a dish with a 1-inch rim. Place on rack over boiling water, cover, and steam 20 minutes or until fish appears white and firm (test its flakiness with a fork). While fish is steaming, make sauce: sliver ginger, garlic, celery, green chilies, onion, green onions and lettuce. Heat a wok, add oil, heat oil. Add sliced ingredients except green onions and lettuce, and brown for 2 minutes. Stir in bean sauce, add water and sugar, and bring to a boil. Mix cornstarch and water, add to sauce and stir until it thickens. Stir in vinegar. Pour sauce over steamed fish. Scatter shredded green onions and lettuce over all. Serve with rice.

Yield: 4 servings.

Note: If you like this hot bean sauce, use it in other recipes where bean sauce is specified.

Crab in Ginger Sauce   CHINA

    8 hard shell blue crabs (each crab yields ½ cup
        meat)
    ¼ cup fresh minced ginger
    3 tablespoons brown sugar
    ¼ cup light soy sauce

3 tablespoons white vinegar
2 green onions
1 head iceberg lettuce.

Preparation: Rinse crabs in water. Fill a sink or large pot with water and dissolve ⅓ cup of salt in it. Transfer crabs to this solution for 30 minutes. Drain and rinse. (This restores some of the fresh taste to the crabs and also cleans the crabs.) Set aside. In a small saucepan, combine minced ginger, brown sugar, light soy sauce, and white vinegar. Set aside. Finely chop green onions and add to sauce pan. Turn heat to low, dissolve sugar, and set aside. Shred lettuce and set on a serving platter.

Cooking: Bring one inch water to boil in one or two large pots with a teaspoon of salt for every quart; put in a few crabs and steam-boil for 20-25 minutes until the shell turns red. Retrieve. Repeat until all crabs are cooked. Replenish the water with boiling water from a kettle whenever necessary. Turn crab on its back, peel off apron and bottom shell. Remove whatever isn't white (though some Chinese eat this bitter orange matter) and discard. Assemble all crabs over bed of lettuce, heat ginger sauce, and pour half over crabs. Put rest in dishes for dipping.

Yield: 4 servings.

Table setting suggestion: Eating whole crabs needs plenty of napkins for the sticky fingers, nutcrackers for the crab legs, and bowls to collect the shells. Plan this recipe for an afternoon party when informality sets the tone. The lettuce ideally contrasts with the salty crab and sweet ginger sauce. A light beer or white wine suits this repast.

Variation: Save crab shells for future use — they can be filled with canned crab meat or crab meat from the fish market, combined with shrimps, and steamed over boiling water 10 minutes to heat. Serve with ginger sauce.

Steamed Flounder CHINA

1 1½ to 2-pound flounder
1 teaspoon salt
3 dried mushrooms
8 lily flowers
1 small pork chop
2 tablespoons sherry
3 slices ginger
2 cloves garlic
¼ cup sliced bamboo shoots
2 green onions
⅓ cup oil
4 tablespoons light soy sauce
1½ teaspoons sugar

Preparation: Wash, scale, and dry fish. Sprinkle with salt and lay on a platter that will fit in a steamer. (The dark side of the fish faces up.) Soak mushrooms and lily flowers in water for 20 minutes; slice the mushrooms into thin strips and tie the lilies into knots. If the ends of the flowers are tough, cut them off. Cut the ginger strips into matchsticks, the garlic into shreds, and the bamboo shoots into strips. Slice the pork into thin pieces and marinate in sherry 15 minutes. Shred green onions into 1-inch lengths. Arrange mushrooms, lily buds, pork strips, ginger, garlic, and bamboo shoots over fish.

Cooking: Set plate on steaming rack, cover, and cook 25-30 minutes. Make the sauce while the fish is steaming. In a small saucepan dissolve sugar in oil and soy. Bring sauce to a boil before removing the plate from the steamer. Cover fish with sauce, garnish with green onions, and serve.

Yield: 4 servings.

Comments: A beautiful sight and a sweet-tasting fish. Two flounders will not fit on one plate, since the fish is flat and wide. Substitute two trouts or whitings for more servings. You may also omit pork strips in favor of cooked ham pieces to be added at the end.

THAILAND
Fish in Banana-leaf Cup

   1 pound fillets of fish (fillets of sole; flounder fillets)
   2 teaspoons *keang som* (red curry paste)
   1 tablespoon fish sauce
   1 cup coconut milk
   1 egg, slightly beaten
   1 green onion
   1 red chili
   banana leaves
   thin toothpicks

Garnish:
   red chilies
   green onions

Preparation: Cut the fillets in strips, then slice crosswise. Place in a medium-size bowl and pound with a wooden spoon to a consistency like mashed potatoes. Set aside. Crumble *keang som* over fish and mix well. Add fish sauce, coconut milk, and egg. Finely shred green onion and red chili. Mince together. Combine with fish. Set aside.

Making cups: Cut banana leaves into 7-inch circles. With your hands, make a pleat to form a corner out of the circle. Secure with a thin toothpick (a thicker one will split the leaf and the mixture will leak). Make three other pleats — you now have a banana cup! Construct three more of these. Spoon fish paste to fill cups three-fourths full. Place banana holders on a plate.

Steaming: Bring water to a boil in steamer, set dish on rack, cover, and steam for 30 minutes.

Retrieve, move cups to another platter. Allow to cool slightly. For garnish, sliver red chilies and green onions into threads ½-inch long. Sprinkle over white fish. Serve.

Yield: 4 servings.

Possibilities: Delicious chilled. Can be prepared early in the day, cooled, wrapped in plastic, and chilled.

Shopping hint: Only the best leaves will make the cups. Old or split leaves crack when toothpicks lance them; then the coconut milk and egg run out onto the plate. The leaf taste is essential to this recipe; if your banana leaves aren't suitable for making cups, use parts of the banana leaf to line four 4½-inch custard dishes, cover with fish, and steam 30 minutes. Garnish, serve at room temperature or chilled.

Tumeric Fish (Nga Baung Doke)   BURMA

   1½ pounds fish fillets (flounder fillet; fillet of sole)
   salt
   tumeric
   1 large onion
   5 cloves garlic
   4 slices ginger, the size of quarters
   2 red chilies
   ½ cup fresh coconut crumbs
   2 tablespoons sesame oil
   2 teaspoons rice flour
   banana leaves
   4-6 cabbage leaves
   coriander leaves

Preparation: Divide fillets into equal portions.

Sprinkle lightly with pepper, salt, and tumeric. Coarsely chop, then finely mince onion, garlic, ginger, and chilies. Place in a medium bowl, add chili powder, fresh coconut, sesame oil, and rice flour. Mix well. Set aside. Cut banana leaves into four strips, rinse, and wipe excess water off. Wash cabbage leaves, dry, and place on top of rinsed banana leaves. Dip fish in onion mixture and place on cabbage leaf. Spoon some mixture to surround the fillet, sprinkle a few coriander leaves over all, and wrap cabbage leaf tightly around fish. Fold banana leaf over cabbage leaf, tie with string or lance with toothpick to close.

Cooking: Place packets directly on steamer rack over boiling water, cover, and steam 25 minutes. (For an improvised steamer, set package on a plate over boiling water.) Retrieve. Serve fish in leaves with white rice. Do not eat banana leaves.

Yield: 4 servings.

Custom: Burmese and Tahitians wrap food in two and sometimes three different leaves. Usually an inedible one — banana, bamboo, *ti*, palm — encloses an edible leaf of spinach, *bok choy*, mustard green, lettuce, or cabbage.

Tip: If your banana leaves won't fold without cracking, use aluminum foil to envelop the leaf and the fish. The effect is the same as making a leaf package.

Oysters in Oyster Sauce   CHINA

> 12 fresh oysters
> 2 teaspoons cornstarch
> 1 tablespoon water
> 2 tablespoons oil
> 2 cloves garlic
> 3 slices ginger
> 5 tablespoons oyster sauce

Garnish:
> green onions

Preparation: Wash oysters — soak them first in cold water for 20 minutes if they are especially sandy. Drain and place in a deep dish.

Steaming: Bring a pot of water to boil in the steamer, set plate on platform, cover and steam 20 minutes. While oysters are cooking, mix cornstarch and water into a smooth liquid. Set aside. Slice garlic and ginger. Shred green onions and set aside. Retrieve and drain oysters.

Stir-frying: Heat wok, add and heat oil. Brown ginger and garlic. Add drained oysters and stir-fry 2 minutes. Stir in oyster sauce and cook 2 minutes. Remove. Garnish with green onions.

Yield: 4 servings.

Shopping tip: ½ lb. of oysters yields 12-14 small oysters. A 10-oz. jar usually contains a dozen. If you purchase a jar which has only four or five large oysters, chop them up after steaming.

Shrimp in Lobster Sauce   CHINA

> 1½ pounds medium or large shrimp
> 2 teaspoons cornstarch
> 1 teaspoon oil
> 1 pork chop
> 3 cloves garlic
> 4 slices ginger
> 1 tablespoon *dow see* (fermented salted black beans)
> 2 tablespoons light soy sauce
> 2 eggs, slightly beaten
> 1 green onion

Preparation: Shell and de-vein shrimp. Dry and place in a deep heatproof plate with a rim. Sprinkle cornstarch over shrimp and work it into the shrimp with your fingers. Add oil and do the same. Set aside. Slice pork chop into thin strips, 1 inch long. Set aside. Sliver and mince garlic and ginger. Set aside. Rinse *dow see* in water. Combine with garlic and ginger, mash thoroughly with mortar and pestle or on the chopping block with wooden handle of cleaver. Transfer to a small bowl, add soy and beaten eggs. Stir in pork strips. Pour over shrimp.

Cooking: Set plate on steaming rack over boiling water, cover, and steam 10 minutes — shrimp tastes juicy and looks plump. If shrimps are in a tight curl, they cooked too long and will feel tough. Serve warm with rice and something fried or stir-fried.

Yield: 4 servings.

Leftover: Add cold sauce and shrimp to stir-fried broccoli at the last minute, heat , and serve. Instant sauce!

Shrimp tips: When buying shrimp, look for bright and clear orange shells. Light-colored shrimp with a faint orange or pink tinge have a mushy texture. Remove all the shells at once, de-vein shrimps at one time, and wash all at once. This assembly-line method saves time; you don't have to turn on the faucet each time to rinse the dirt from the vein. A sharp cleaver can de-vein and butterfly (i.e., cut the shrimp almost through) faster than a small knife. After the shrimp have been shelled, lay one on cutting board. Hold shrimp lightly by resting three fingers on it. With the tip of the cleaver, gently make one deep cut. Do not curve the blade around the body of the shrimp; the vein usually doesn't extend that far. With a little practice, de-veining shrimp becomes no effort at all.

Note: You may have noticed that black bean seasoning is often used to steam, stir-fry, and bake Chinese dishes. The Chinese never tire of it, because it flavors all meats differently. It can be made mild or pungent — everybody finds how much they like and employ it often. It's most commonly used with lobster; hence it has become known as "lobster sauce."

Fish with Steak Sauce   CHINA

1 1½-2 pound whole fish (black bass)
sherry
salt
2 tablespoons steak sauce
1 teaspoon worcestershire sauce
2 tablespoons oyster sauce
1 tablespoon light soy sauce
1 tablespoon bean sauce
2 teaspoons sugar
½ teaspoon salt
4 cloves garlic
4 slices fresh ginger
3 green chilies
2 green onions
3 tablespoons oil

Preparation: Rinse fish with sherry. Score both sides of fish, lightly salt. Place on a plate with a rim.

Cooking: Set dish on platform over boiling water, cover, and steam 20-25 minutes until firm (look for a pool of liquid surrounding the fish as a sign it's done). While fish is steaming, make sauce: in a small bowl, mix steak, worcestershire, oyster, light soy, bean sauces, sugar, and salt. Slice garlic, ginger, and green chilies; mince together. Shred green onions (save one stalk for garnish). Combine all chopped ingredients with sauce. Heat oil in a saucepan, pour in contents of bowl, and bring to a boil, stirring constantly.

Serving: Retrieve fish. Pour sauce over fish, garnish with green onions, and serve with rice, a fried dish, and steamed vegetables such as yard beans, heart of *bok choy*, yams, or corn.

Yield: 4 servings.

Possibility: This sauce is thicker than the usual sauces over steamed fish and therefore goes well with a fried or baked fish, too.

CHINA
Chopped Crab & Salted Egg

> 1 large crab
> salt
> 2 small pork chops
> 2 cloves garlic
> 3 slices ginger
> 4 water chestnuts
> 1 tablespoon *dow see* (fermented salted black
>   beans)
> 1 salted egg.

Preparation: Rinse crab in cold water. Remove its apron and shell. Discard. Take out all beige matter. The orange part is edible though bitter. With the back edge of a cleaver, crack the crab legs in several places so that nut crackers will not be needed later on. Now divide the body in two and chop each section into three parts connected with a crab leg. Arrange in a deep plate. Lightly salt. Set aside. Bone the pork chops (freeze bones for soup stock). Cut the pork into strips, then dice and mince. Place in a medium-sized bowl. Chop coarsely individually and mince together: garlic, ginger, and water chestnuts. Set aside. Rinse *dow see* in water. Place in a small bowl, add garlic mixture, and mash well with heel of cleaver. Combine with pork mixture. Set aside. Scrape the black ash caked around the salted egg. Rinse and break into meat mixture, but take out the hardened egg yolk before stirring pork. Pour over crab. Cut yolk into 6 pieces and flatten with the cleaver. Decorate each section of the crab with yolk.

Cooking: Bring water to a boil, set plate on platform, cover, and steam 20 minutes. Once during steaming, loosen crab from the plate with a fork — this action mixes the crab juices with the black bean and pork flavors.

Yield: 4 servings.

Variation: 1) Include a few chopped green or red chillies before steaming. 2) Use a bottled chili sauce from Thailand to sprinkle over crab meat and as a dip for a Southeast Asian flavor.

Uses of salted egg: The egg white thickens minced meats in place of cornstarch; the bright yellow of the yolk contributes to the pleasing appearance of chopped crab and stuffed bitter melons.

Lobster variation: Use lobster tails instead of crab. Loosen meat from shell but leave in shell. Arrange in a deep dish. Follow all other directions. Seafood and minced meat combine well.

Crispy Onion Fish   MALAYSIA

1 2-pound white fish (trout)
sherry
1 small onion
1 green chili
½ cup oil
6 tablespoons light soy sauce

Preparation: Wash, scale, and dry fish. Rinse with some sherry and lay in a plate. Make a few diagonal cuts on both sides of the fish (to allow seasonings in). Slice onion into ⅛-inch wedges and mince green chili.

Cooking: Set plate on steaming rack. Cover and steam 20 minutes. Five minutes before the fish is cooked, heat oil in a small pan. Brown onion and chili until the wedges look like crispy black threads. Add soy (let the splatter die down) and pour over fish. Serve warm with rice and curry. This is a spicy recipe which becomes spicier with more minced chilies.

Yield: 4 servings.

Variation: Substitute shallots for onions for a crunchier and more seasoned taste. These exotic purple onions which peel like garlic can be found in speciality shops and some groceries.

Historical note: The original Malay foods and manners resembled the Pacific islands' diet of coconuts, bananas, fresh fruit, fish, and pork. Eating with fingers was the customary practice; these foods did not require utensils or chopsticks. Today, Malays all use a spoon and fork except for the old guard, who regard such articles as unclean since they are used again. (Banana leaf plates were always thrown away, coconut shells eventually tossed out.) The right hand holds the spoon, the left the fork; it's the fork that pushes the food onto the spoon whence the food is eaten. The spoon also gets the gravy and rice.

Serving suggestion: Present day Malaysia combines the cultures of China, Indonesia (homeland of the original Malays), and India; consequently most residents cook several cuisines, adapting recipes to their whim. Sheila Lee Hancock is the source for my Crispy Onion Fish; it has a Chinese base of soy and hot oil with Indonesian and Indian overtones of the spicy chilies and black onions. For an elaborate meal, serve all dishes at one time. These may include an Indian chicken and vegetable curry, assorted chutneys (fruit sauces), Crispy Onion Fish, an Indonesian *satay* (barbecued skewered meat), raw and steamed vegetables, *sambals* (fried side dishes), and white rice. For dessert, slice oranges.

HAWAII & TAHITI

Coconut Fish in Ti Leaves

2 pounds fish steaks
salt
pepper
¼ pound salt pork
1 coconut
4 *ti* leaves
1 lemon

Preparation: Wash, scale, and dry fish, if necessary. Season both sides with salt and pepper. Set aside. Slice salt pork into thin strips, cutting off excess fat. Set aside. Open coconut (see "Fresh Coconut Milk"), scrape out meat. Put pieces in blender with 1 cup water and liquify (it may take several steps to do this — start with the "whip" setting). Lay aside. Slice lemons into thin circles, and then into halves. Set aside. Rinse *ti* leaves with water and drain off water. With a small knife loosen top of stem and pull to peel off rigid stem. Place fish on leaf, pour ¼ cup coconut milk over fish, arrange a few lemon slices on top, and roll leaf to its end. Wrap with aluminum foil.

Steaming: Lay silver packets directly on steamer rack (and not piled atop each other) over boiling water. Cover and steam 25 minutes.

Yield: 4 servings.

Serving: Place parcels in a large bowl decorated with fresh banana and *ti* leaves, more lemon slices, and banana flowers, sometimes eaten as a vegetable. An empty bowl to collect the leaves keeps the table clean. Have coconut cups filled with iced water and set in *ti* or bamboo leaf holders.

Variation: Use lean bacon if salt pork is not

available. Lay packages of fish on a plate over boiling water if steamer tray isn't used.

Comments: Hawaiian, Tahitian, and Samoan meals are similar (at one time the natives probably were all related, but some canoed north to Hawaii and other islands and settled). Breadfruit, leaf-wrapped chicken and fish dishes, sweet potatoes, coconuts, pork, much fresh fruit (bananas, papayas, figs, tamarinds) exemplify the Polynesian diet. Hawaiians pound the taro root into *poi* with the consistency of pudding, whereas the Tahitians eat it like a potato. The Hawaiians like their breadfruit riper. The Tahitian roast pig is crispy, the Hawaiian mushy. In Polynesia, mullet is a favorite choice for coconut fish. The fresh coconut flavor elevates this simply seasoned dish to a marvelous experience.

Thai Fish Cake (Pla Nerng)　　THAILAND

1 pound fish fillets (fillets of sole)
1 teaspoon salt
1 red chili
4 cloves garlic
1 onion
2 stalks fresh coriander (leaves, stalks, and roots)

¼ teaspoon ground tumeric
¼ teaspoon ground peper
2 tablespoons fish sauce
½ cup frozen coconut milk
1 egg, slightly beaten
banana leaf
2 teaspoons rice flour

Preparation: Lightly salt the fillet(s), slice into ½-inch crosswise sections, and set aside. Chop coarsely, then mince together: chili, garlic, onion, and coriander. Place in medium-sized bowl. Add tumeric, pepper, fish sauce, and 2 tablespoons of the thawed coconut milk, and half of beaten egg. Stir well, add fish slices, and coat. Set aside. Cut one banana leaf the size of a deep glass pie pan, the other leaf one inch larger. Line plate with the big leaf. Place bright yellow fish fillet slices on this green-leaf bed, forming a neat circle. Mix remaining coconut milk with rice flour, and pour over fish cake but not into the banana leaf. Lightly press smaller leaf on top of fish.

Cooking: Bring water to a boil, put plate on steaming rack, cover, and steam 25 minutes. Serve at room temperature with rice, Spicy Pork Coins, and a raw cabbage and cucumber salad with the same dip.

Yield: 4 servings.

Possibilities: When chilled, this fish cake can be used as canapé spread. Or make, refrigerate, and serve as cold main dish the next day.

Comment: Two different flavors when served at different temperatures. Use any available fillets — redfish or trout — but bone first. Fillets of sole and flounder fillets don't need any preparation.

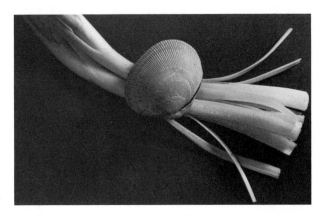

Clams with Green Onions   JAPAN

1 can clams
2 bunches green onions

Miso sauce:
½ cup roasted peanuts
¼ cup *miso*
3 tablespoons sugar
5 tablespoons vinegar
1 tablespoon clam juice

Preparation: Drain clams (save juice). Chop green onions into 1-inch pieces. Combine with clams in a pie pan. Make *miso* sauce: grind peanuts in mortar and pestle or crush with wooden handle of a cleaver, add *miso,* and mash well. Blend in sugar, vinegar, and clam juice. Set aside.

Steaming: Place dish over boiling water, cover, and steam 3 minutes. Retrieve, drain dish.

Serving: Pour sauce over green onions and clams. Serve immediately.

Yield: 4 servings.

Variations: Substitute canned abalone or boiled fresh cuttlefish for clams.

INSTANT FISH

Canned salmon and tuna when steamed make fast and nutritious side dishes for all cuisines. With a few garnishes and some seasoning, canned salmon or tuna can have a Chinese, Japanese, or Thai Flavor.

Preparation: Open a 7 or 8-ounce can of tuna or salmon. Drain some juice and place fish on a small dish.

Cooking: Steam alongside the rice for 15 minutes. Serve warm or at room temperature.

Japanese seasoning: drizzle 1 tablespoon Japanese soy sauce over fish before steaming. Make a dip of 1 tablespoon of soy and few dashes *aji* (monosodium glutamate).

Chinese seasoning: add 2 teaspoons of light soy sauce and a few ginger threads and green onions over salmon or tuna before steaming.

Thai seasoning: mix 1 tablespoon of fish sauce and 2 stalks of chopped fresh coriander with salmon or tuna. Garnish with fried garlic slivers.

Korean seasoning: make a paste of 1 tablespoon toasted sesame seeds, 1 teaspoon sugar, and 2 tablespoons light soy sauce. Spread over tuna and steam.

Vietnamese seasoning: mix 1 teaspoon fish sauce, 1 teaspoon light soy sauce over fish. Steam and pour 2 tablespoons coconut cream on top. Garnish with green onion.

Malaysian seasoning: add chopped chilies and grated ginger before steaming. Squeeze lemon juice over, if desired.

Indian seasoning: spoon some yogurt and chopped tomatoes over fish before steaming. Garnish with mint leaves.

Polynesian seasoning: slice a few pieces of salt pork or lean bacon. Mix with 2 tablespoons coconut cream, dashes of salt and pepper, and pour over fish. Steam.

Burmese seasoning: fry 1/8 teaspoon of shrimp paste, 1/4 chopped onion, 1 clove minced garlic in teaspoon of oil. Pour over fish. Steam.

Seasoning of Sri Lanka: Sprinkle tuna with tumeric. Steam. Garnish with chopped onions, garlic slices, and chopped tomatoes cooked in a little oil and 1/4 teaspoon chili powder.

vegetables

The vitamins in vegetables are water soluble. The less liquid used to cook them, the more nutritious they remain. Steamed vegetables advantageously retain shape, color, and texture close to their raw state. Asians stuff chilies, mushrooms, peppers, and zucchini with meat, which makes the dish a light meal with rice or a substantial side serving. Plain steamed vegetables are eaten with dips and sauces; each country has at least one.

Steamed vegetables can be prepared in two ways: 1) vegetables are placed on a plate and cooked in a covered steamer over boiling water, or 2) the vegetables simmer and steam in ½ inch of boiling water, yogurt, or soup. Vegetables should be sliced for faster cooking. Pork is the favorite minced filling, but you can replace it with turkey, beef, chicken, shrimp, or fish. Mincing the meat instead of grinding it produces a finer texture. Ground meat feels compact and flavors unevenly, though it is convenient. Refer to page 5 for mincing hints.

Steamed vegetables and raw vegetables can be combined or served separately. Indonesia's *gado gado* with a peanut sauce mixes raw cucumbers and lettuce with steamed green beans and boiled potatoes. A side dish of steamed spinach accompanies Korea's *kim chee* (pickled vinegared cabbage) and Japan's *sunomono* (vinegared vegetable salad). Polynesians eat plenty of raw fruits and coconuts and steam sweet potatoes and bananas. Vegetables provide the necessary fiber in Asian diets.

Pearl Mushrooms (Song-I Busut Jim)   KOREA

20 fresh mushrooms (1½'' diameter)
1¼ cup raw chicken
15 water chestnuts
3 slices fresh ginger
4 green onions
¼ cup sliced bamboo shoots
1 tablespoon cornstarch
1 tablespoon light soy sauce
2 teaspoons oyster sauce
½ teaspoon salt

Preparation: Wash and dry mushrooms. Remove stems (use for soup or stir-fry). Mince chicken. Set aside. Slice water chestnuts. Shred ginger slices and green onions. Finely chop water chestnuts, ginger slices, green onions, and sliced bamboo shoots. Combine with chicken and mix well with your hands. Add cornstarch, light soy sauce, oyster sauce, and salt. Stir well. Fill mushroom caps with a tablespoon of chicken. Lightly shape the filling into a mound. Oil a plate with ½ teaspoon vegetable oil and set mushrooms on it. Place plate on rack over boiling water.

Cooking and Serving: Steam 20 minutes in a covered steamer. Remove, spoon mushroom juices over mixture. Serve at room temperature.

Yield: 4 servings.

Possibility: Use as an appetizer. Transfer chicken

balls to another plate and insert toothpicks in the center of the mushrooms for easy handling.

Shopping tips: With raw chicken meat. breasts are the easiest parts to de-bone (or you can purchase boneless breasts). Choose mushrooms that are closed around the stem (so you can't see the dark brown yet); they stay fresher than those already opened. Prepare filled mushrooms ahead of time, refrigerate, and cook when you are ready to serve; Pearl Mushrooms do not reheat to advantage — eat them all up.

SAMOA, TAHITI, HAWAII

Steamed Bananas

> 3 ripe yellow-colored plantains
>   (cooking bananas)
> butter
> salt
> pepper
> banana leaves

Preparation: Peel bananas with a knife. Rinse banana leaves with water and cut into long pieces. Place banana on leaf, season with butter, salt, and pepper, roll leaf, and secure open ends with thin toothpicks.

Cooking: Place directly on steaming racks, cover, and steam 30 minutes. Remove from leaf and slice in half, one banana for two people.

Yield: 6 servings.

Notes: A riper cooking banana may require only 20 minutes. Bananas that can be eaten as fruit are not recommended for cooking because they are too soft. Green plantains are hard like a potato, taste like a potato, and are used as a starch vegetable in

Hawaiian and Tahitian meals. Allow a week for green bananas to ripen. For a variation, you can slice the bananas into long thin pieces and fry on both sides in a tablespoon of oil. Remove, flatten with a spatula, return the slices to the oil, and cook a little longer — they should be very crispy like French fries. Boiling or steaming an unpeeled banana takes twice as much time, since you must cook it until the skin bursts. Plantains that are too green become gummy after steaming. It's better to fry these. Many cooking bananas available in the United States come from Costa Rica. They vary from the familiar banana shape with tapered ends to a thick cucumber shape with rounded ends.

Lamb-Stuffed Bell Peppers   INDIA (Mirchi Bharwan)

> 4 medium-sized bell peppers
> 1 cup lamb
> ½ onion
> 1 chili
> 1 tablespoon ground coriander
> ¼ cup long-grain rice (Basmati)
> ½ teaspoon sugar
> 1 teaspoon salt
> 2 teaspoons lemon juice
> 1 teaspoon grated lemon peel

Preparation: With a sharp knife, cut around the stalk of the pepper. Remove stalk, pith, and seeds. Save stalk to top pepper later. Mince lamb. Set aside. Finely chop onion and chili. Combine with lamb and rice. Mix thoroughly with ground coriander, sugar, salt, lemon juice, and lemon peel. Fill pepper lightly (the rice becomes fluffy during steaming) and cover with its stem.

Cooking: Bring half a pot of water to boil, lower heat, stand peppers in the liquid, and simmer 45 minutes. Serve warm or at room temperature.

Yield: 4 servings.

Tips: The water in the pot should not be higher than half way up the sides of the pepper or it will boil into the filling. I buy a lamb shank, which is enough for this recipe. You may substitute minced beef, which steams better than ground beef. This is a simple, superb side dish; serve in small portions with rice, another vegetable, a curry, and cucumbers in yogurt. In India all portions are small except for rice, the main food.

Spinach with Toasted Sesame Seed Sauce   JAPAN

    1 pound fresh spinach
    2 tablespoons sesame seeds
    2 tablespoons Japanese soy sauce
    1 tablespoon sugar

Preparation: Wash spinach thoroughly. Chop in 2-inch pieces and spread on a plate. Toast sesame seeds in a dry pan, remove, and pulverize with mortar and pestle or wooden handle of a knife. Add to soy, pour in sugar.

Cooking: Steam spinach in a covered steamer for 5-6 minutes until limp yet bright green. Remove. Stir in sesame seed mixture and toss evenly. Serve warm or cold.

Yield: 4 servings.

Cooking hint: If you plan to serve this dish chilled, do not add sauce. Use sauce as a dip. Grains of sand imbedded in the stalks and leaves can ruin this dish; best solution: immerse spinach in water for 10 minutes before washing.

Vegetable variations: Steam ½ head of shredded cabbage 15 minutes; cut string beans 35 minutes; bean sprouts 3 minutes; and watercress 5 minutes. If served warm, stir sauce through vegetable. If served chilled, sauce becomes a dip.

Additional idea: Rinse 4 spinach leaves, place one on a *sudare* (wooden mat), put ½ cup steamed watercress on leaf, and roll *sudare* to make a firm cylinder of watercress. Remove and repeat. Chill rolls, slice into ½-inch pieces and place cut side up on a plate (like *norimaki sushi*). Serve with dip.

Stuffed Bitter Melon   CHINA

    3 small bitter melons (*foo gwa*)
    2 teaspoons *dow see* (fermented salted black beans)
    ½ cup raw pork
    5 water chestnuts
    2 stalks green onions
    1 teaspoon cornstarch
    ½ teaspoon salt

Preparation: Halve and seed bitter melons. Boil the water in the steamer, blanch the vegetables for two minutes, and set aside. (Keep the water boiling since the mincing won't take long.) Rinse the black beans in water, mash well, and set aside. Mince pork. Set aside. Finely chop water chestnuts and green onions. Add to pork. Stir in cornstarch, salt, and black beans. Mix thoroughly and pat into empty shells.

Cooking: Set melon halves on a plate. Steam covered 30 minutes. Retrieve plate and spoon the vegetable juice over the pork.

Yield: 4 servings.

Serving suggestion: Serve warm. Complements bland dishes and fried foods.

Comments: If any vegetable can flavor meat (instead of vice versa), *foo gwa* is that vegetable. Like most Chinese children, I did not like the taste of bitter melon; I ate all the meat that it touched, however. The sharp, ascerbic flavor is truly Oriental; it usually requires repeated samplings to appreciate this vegetable.

Variation: Cut melon rings ½-inch wide, core and seed. Scrape the black-ash covering off a salted egg, rinse and break into a bowl, separating the hard yolk from the runny egg white. Mix the white with the pork mixture. Place empty rings on a plate. Fill with pork. Quarter the yolk and flatten with the blade of a cleaver. Cut in half and place a yellow section on top of each pork-filled melon medallion. Place dish on rack over boiling water. Cover and steam 25 minutes. Serve warm or at room temperature. A lovely tempting recipe.

Variation: Make a paste of 2 teaspoons mashed black beans and 1 clove minced garlic. Set aside. Make a cornstarch binder of ¾ cup stock or water and 2 teaspoons cornstarch. Set aside. Substitute ½ cup of fillet of sole for the pork. Omit black beans. Cut the melon in 1-inch rings instead of halves, seed, and fill with mashed fish mixture. Carefully fry in 2 tablespoons oil until fish is dark brown on both sides. Lower heat, add black bean and garlic paste, stir for 15 seconds. Pour in cornstarch liquid, cover, and steam 15 minutes, adding more water if sauce looks too thick. Transfer fish cakes to a plate and cover with sauce. Serve warm with white rice.

Vegetable Salad (Gado-Gado)   INDONESIA

1 pound fresh spinach
8 yard beans
2 cups bean sprouts
2 small new potatoes
2 cups oil

Garnish:

1 cucumber
½ head iceberg lettuce

Sauce:

1 small onion
1 clove garlic
2 slices ginger root
3 red chilies
¼ teaspoon shrimp paste
1 tablespoon oil
1 cup water
½ cup fresh coconut shreds or crumbs
½ cup unsalted roasted peanuts, chopped
4 tablespoons brown sugar
¼ cup frozen or canned coconut milk
juice of 1 lime

Preparation: Rinse vegetables, carefully wash sand from spinach, scrub potatoes. Cut yard beans into 2-inch lengths. Chop spinach coarsely. Place yard beans, spinach, and bean sprouts in separate plates.

Cooking: Bring water to a boil in the steamer pot and drop potatoes in to cook 30 minutes. On top racks, steam yard beans 30 minutes, spinach 8 minutes, and bean sprouts 4 minutes. Remove vegetables. Set aside. Retrieve potatoes, allow to cool, and dice into ½-inch cubes. Heat a wok, add oil, heat oil. When hot, deep-fry potatoes for 5-8 minutes until golden brown. Remove and blot on paper towels. Set aside. Make garnish: slice cucumber into ¼-inch circles; shred lettuce. Shape a bed of lettuce and overlap the cucumber pieces around the edge of the plate; place the spinach in one row, the potatoes next to it, then the yard beans, then the bean sprouts. Set aside.

Making sauce: Dice onion, mince garlic, sliver ginger and chilies into threads. In wok, heat 1 tablespoon oil, add onion, garlic, ginger, chilies, and shrimp paste. Stir and watch for onion to become transparent. Add water and cook at a medium boil for 5 minutes. Add fresh coconut, roasted peanuts, brown sugar. Lower heat, stir in coconut milk and lime juice. Turn off heat and pour into several bowls from which people can spoon sauce.

Yield: 6 servings.

Serving: Set salad in the center of the table. If you made the sauce previously, let it come to room temperature or warm before serving.

Shopping tip: For this recipe, the brown-colored shrimp paste that comes in small plastic jars is preferable to the purplish shrimp paste popular in the Philippines and China. Another thing: yard beans are thinner and darker green and more tender than string beans. Use fresh string beans if yard beans are not available, and steam 35 minutes.

Cooking hint: The shrimp paste employed in this sauce is a powerful-smelling potion whose aroma lingers in the air for hours. It's advisable to make the sauce a day or two beforehand and refrigerate it. The salad itself, however, should be made the same day.

THAILAND
Green Chilies in Egg

4 long yellow or green chili peppers (6 inches)
¾ cup raw pork
2 stalks coriander
2 cloves garlic
¼ onion
1 teaspoon pepper
½ teaspoon salt
2 eggs, slightly beaten
1 tablespoon oil

Garnish:
coriander leaves

Preparation: Slice chili in half, remove seeds and pith. Set aside. Mince pork. Set aside. Finely chop coriander, garlic, and onion. Combine with pork and add pepper, salt, and a quarter of the beaten eggs. Save the rest to make egg nets. Fill empty shells and set on a plate.

Cooking: Place plate on steaming rack over boiling water, cover, steam 10 minutes. Meanwhile, heat the wok on medium; add oil around its sides. With a pair of chopsticks, drip strings of egg across the bowl of the wok in all directions. Let cook, remove with chopsticks, drain on paper towels, and repeat until egg is used up. Retrieve chilies. Form a net of these yellow and brown-colored threads over the stuffed chilies. Sprinkle with coriander leaves to make a colorful dish. Serve warm or at room temperature.

Yield: 4 servings.

Garnishes: Green onions and red chilies may also decorate this dish. To make the green onion curls, cut off two inches of green above the white part of the onion. With the tip of a knife or cleaver make seven or eight lengthwise cuts from the bottom of the white through ends of the green. Put shredded onion in iced water — the green ends will curl backwards in a few minutes to form the fronds of a small palm tree. Red chili flowers are made on the same principle, except make fewer cuts (5 or 6) for the petals to curl in the water. Only the most practiced palate will be able to eat a red chili flower — they feel 10 times hotter than a jalapeño. Decorate all Thai dishes except desserts with green onion fronds and red chili flowers.

Variation: Deep fry stuffed chilies 2 minutes in 2 cups oil after steaming. Blot with paper towels. Garnish with green onions and chilies.

SZECHWAN PROVINCE
CHINA

Szechwan Spinach

    1 pound fresh spinach
    ¼ cup dried shrimp
    ½ teaspoon chili oil
    1 teaspoon sesame seed paste
    1 tablespoon rice vinegar
    1 teaspoon light soy sauce

Preparation: Cover spinach with water for 10 minutes to loosen dirt and small grains of sand, then wash carefully. Chop in 2-inch pieces and lay in a deep dish. Soak dried shrimps for 1 hour or until soft, chop into smaller pieces, and set aside. In a small bowl mix chili oil, sesame seed paste, rice vinegar, and light soy sauce.

Cooking: Steam spinach in covered steamer 5-6 minutes. Heat a sauce pan, add 1 teaspoon oil, and brown shrimp for 30 seconds. Stir in sesame seed mixture. Keep warm until spinach is ready. Pour over spinach, mixing vegetable juices with sauce. Serve warm.

Yield: 4 servings.

Comment: A mildly spicy recipe. The Szechwan province — famous for its hot foods — would increase the sesame seed paste to 1 tablespoon.

Eggplant in Sesame Sauce   CHINA

    1 medium eggplant
    3 cloves garlic
    3 slices ginger
    1 tablespoon oil
    1 tablespoon sugar
    ¼ teaspoon salt
    2 tablespoons light soy sauce
    1 tablespoon white vinegar
    1 teaspoon sesame oil

Preparation: Wash and cut eggplant into thick wedges and arrange attractively in a deep plate. Do not peel eggplant — the skin is eaten, too.

Cooking: Set plate on rack, cover, and steam 30 minutes. While eggplant is cooking, mince garlic and ginger. Fry in oil until light brown. In a small bowl, mix sugar, soy sauce, vinegar, and sesame oil and stir into hot garlic mixture for a few seconds, until the sugar dissolves. Retrieve eggplant, pour mixture over wedges. Spoon vegetable juices (which contain vitamins) and sauce over eggplant. Serve warm or at room temperature.

Yield: 4 servings.

Variation: If you buy the comparatively tiny Chinese eggplants, use six instead of one and halve each plant. Follow all other directions. A sweet-tasting dish to complement a fried dish.

Stuffed Zucchini THAILAND

> 4 thin zucchinis (7″ long)
> ¼ cup raw pork
> ¼ cup raw chicken
> 3 cloves garlic
> 1 teaspoon fish sauce
> ½ teaspoon pepper

Garnish:
> coriander leaves
> cooked crab meat
> fried garlic strips

Preparation: Wash and cut off the ends of the zucchini. With a ¼ teaspoon measure remove the seeds from its center. Set aside. Mince the pork. Set aside. Mince the chicken. Set aside. Finely chop the garlic. Mix and chop together pork, chicken, and garlic until they are meshed. Add the fish sauce and pepper. Stir well and stuff into the hollow cylinder. Bring two inches of water to boil in a pot, lower heat to simmer, set zucchinis in water, and steam 30 minutes. Remove, slice in half, and serve as a side dish. Garnish with coriander leaves, shredded crab meat, and fried garlic strips.

Yield: 8 servings.

Additional ideas: 1) Substitute 4 cups of stock for water and you have a vegetable soup. Substitute cooked crab meat for chicken. Slice zucchini into 2-inch sections — although the meat shrinks inside the core, it won't fall out. Garnish the soup with coriander leaves and shredded crab meat. Serve with fish cooked on the steamer tray above the soup, and rice heated on a separate tray. 2) Steam the cored zucchini in a covered steamer until it's soft, about 10 minutes. Slice into ½-inch pieces, fill with raw meat mixture and fry in a little oil. Eat as a vegetable or put a few in hot soup. Add a slightly beaten egg to meat mixture. Set aside. Cut zucchini into ½-inch rings, core and seed. Lay on a plate, spoon pork stuffing into the centers. Set dish over boiling water, cover, and steam 25 minutes. Retrieve. Garnish with coriander leaves and fried garlic strips.

Heart of Bok Choy (Choy Sum) CHINA

> 1 bunch of *choy sum* (heart of the *bok choy*)

Sauce:
> 2 tablespoons oyster sauce
> 2 tablespoons light soy sauce
> 1 tablespoon sherry

Preparation: Wash green stalks well, leaving yellow flowers intact. Lay neatly in a decorated plate — all the flowers pointing one way. Mix oyster sauce, light soy sauce, and sherry. Set aside.

Steaming: Bring a pot of water to boil and set platter on rack, cover, and steam 8 minutes. Meanwhile, warm the sauce. Retrieve, pour sauce over vegetables, serve warm or at room temperature.

Yield: 4 servings.

Shopping tip: *Choy sum* is the center of *bok choy*, an Oriental vegetable with white stalks and leafy dark green leaves. In the Chinatowns of San Francisco, Oakland, and Los Angeles, local residents and out-of-towners purchase *choy sum* without the *bok choy* leaves. Elsewhere, one must peel 2 bunches of *bok choy* to get enough hearts for four servings. *Bok choy* is an everyday vegetable, whereas *choy sum* is always the choice for parties and banquets.

Variation: Use the sauce over any steamed green vegetable such as snow peas or yard beans.

Shrimp Paste Sauce for Steamed Vegetables   THAILAND

> 5 red chilies
> 2 cloves garlic
> 1 small onion
> ½ teaspoon shrimp paste
> ½ teaspoon sugar
> 3 tablespoons lemon juice
> 1 tablespoon water

Preparation: Coarsely chop red chilies, garlic, and onion. Transfer to mortar and grind with pestle. Stir in shrimp paste, sugar, lemon juice, and water. Serve in bowls for communal dipping. Refrigerate leftover sauce.

Yield: ½ cup.

Blending tip: Many Asians who own blenders use the utensil to grind spices for curries and mix sauces. The small amount described here won't blend in a large container unless a few tablespoons of water are added to reach the blades.

Variations: Substitute fresh green chilies or soaked dried red chilies in place of fresh red chilies. Be

careful of the "hot" feeling the chilies impart if you handle the skin and seeds much. Do not touch your eyes. Wash hands with soap and water after mincing. The seeds taste even hotter than the skin.

Sesame Seed Sauce for Steamed Vegetables   KOREA

> ¼ cup sesame seeds
> 2 teaspoons sugar
> 2 tablespoons vinegar
> 3 tablespoons light soy sauce
> ½ teaspoon sesame oil

Preparation: Toast sesame seeds in a dry hot pan. Transfer to mortar and partially crush with pestle or wooden handle of knife. Add sugar, vinegar, and light soy sauce. Stir to dissolve sugar. Serve in individual dishes for warm or chilled vegetables.

Yield: ½ cup.

Storage: Refrigerate; when ready to use, allow to come to room temperature for dipping. It's convenient to double the recipe and store the remaining portion in the refrigerator.

Cabbage in Peanut Sauce   JAPAN

> 1 firm cake *tofu* (fresh bean curd)
> 1 *konnyaku* (yam noodle cake)
> ½ teaspoon salt
> ½ head cabbage

Peanut Sauce:
> ½ cup roasted peanuts
> ½ cup *miso* (fermented soybean paste)
> 2 tablespoons sugar

Garnish:

1 tablespoon toasted sesame seeds

Preparation: Boil *tofu* 5 minutes, remove, and squeeze dry in a clean cloth (don't worry about breaking it). Set aside. Cut *konnyaku* in thin strips, place in ungreased pan, and cook over low heat. Add salt, cook 2 minutes longer. Allow to cool. Shred cabbage, spread in deep dish.

Cooking: Bring a pot of water to boil in steamer pot, set plate on rack, cover, and steam 20 minutes. While vegetable is steaming, make sauce. Pulverize roasted peanuts with mortar and pestle or wooden heel of a knife. Add *miso* and sugar. Continue grinding until well-blended. Transfer to a larger bowl, mix in the squeezed *tofu*, mash all together.

Serving: Stir in the cabbage and *konnyaku*. Garnish with toasted sesame seeds. Serve immediately.

Yield: 4 servings.

Variations: Steamed string beans (35 minutes) or steamed watercress (5 minutes) can be substituted for cabbage. Do not mix vegetable and peanut sauce until you are ready to eat. Refrigerate each separately if prepared a few hours beforehand.

Shopping tip: Buy *miso* in plastic tubs (some have no preservatives). Transfer to a clean air-tight glass jar and refrigerate. It lasts for many months. Japanese use *miso* in soups and sauces. Red-colored *miso* tastes saltier than the white-colored one and most Japanese prefer it.

VEGETABLES: A SUMMARY

Steam Oriental and Western vegetables over boiling water in the steamer pot. Place the main vegetable in a deep dish, garnish with bean sprouts, celery matchsticks, chopped onions, carrot matchsticks, sliced bamboo shoots, bell pepper bits, quartered fresh mushrooms, water chestnuts, sliced dried mushrooms, or broccoli flowers. Don't overload on the variety of vegetables; three is enough. Contrast white and light green vegetables with red, orange, or dark green ones. Season with brown sugar, salt, or pepper before steaming. Use any dip or sauce — sesame seed, peanut, *miso* — for steamed vegetables.

When steaming a main dish and a vegetable dish, position the one that takes the longest time (usually the meat) nearest the water. At some point reverse the levels of meat and vegetables — otherwise the vegetables won't cook fully.

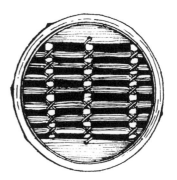

Guide To Steaming Vegetables

VEGETABLE	PREPARATION	STEAMING TIME*
ACORN SQUASH	*Halve and seed. Wet core with water. Place cut side down on plate.*	*Steam 40 minutes for ½ lb. vegetable, 60 minutes for 1 lb. squash.*
ASPARAGUS	*Slice into diagonal ¼-inch thick pieces.*	*Steam 4 minutes.*
BOK CHOY	*Cut stalk in 1-inch pieces, leaves in 1-inch wide strips.*	*Steam 5 minutes.*
BROCCOLI	*Cut stalk into 1-inch by ¼-inch thick planks, flowers into 1-inch pieces. Blanch 2 minutes in boiling water.*	*Steam 8 minutes.*
BUTTERNUT SQUASH	*Do not peel. Seed and cut into ½-inch slices.*	*Steam 30 minutes.*
CARROTS	*Peel and slice into ¼-inch diagonal pieces or matchsticks.*	*Steam 10 minutes.*
CAULIFLOWER	*Cut into 1-inch pieces. Blanch 2 minutes in boiling water.*	*Steam 8 minutes.*
CHINESE CABBAGE	*Shred.*	*Steam 15 minutes.*
CORN ON THE COB	*Remove husk. Break in serving pieces or leave whole.*	*Steam 30-40 minutes.*
KOHLRABI	*Peel. Slice in ¼-inch pieces.*	*Steam 20 minutes.*

VEGETABLE	PREPARATION	STEAMING TIME*
LETTUCE	*Shred.*	*Steam 15 minutes.*
MUSTARD GREENS	*Cut in 2-inch pieces.*	*Steam 15 minutes.*
OKRA	*Stem and cut in 1-inch pieces or leave whole.*	*Steam 20-30 minutes.*
PUMPKIN	*Core.*	*Steam 1 hour for 1 lb. vegetable.*
SNOW PEAS	*Although many people (and most restaurants) don't bother, the snow pea can be made more tender by removing the tough strings that run along its outer edges. To do this, break off the tip of its stem and pull away the strings from its sides. Cut large pods diagonally in half or thirds.*	*Steam 5 minutes. Small flat pods cook in 1 minute.*
SWEET POTATOES	*Peel and cut in 1-inch cubes.*	*Steam 40-50 minutes.*
SWISS CHARD	*Cut stalk in ½-inch diagonal pieces, leaves in 1-inch wide strips.*	*Steam 5 minutes.*
WHITE POTATOES	*Scrub and cut in 1-inch squares or ½-inch slices.*	*Steam 40-50 minutes.*
YAMS	*Peel and cut into ½-inch slices.*	*Steam 40-50 minutes.*
ZUCCHINI	*Cut into ¼-inch slices.*	*Steam 5 minutes.*

Steaming time for vegetables cooking on the lower tray of an aluminum steamer.

soups - a gentle affair

One hears little about steamed soups; boiled soups are more universal. Yet steamed soups extract the flavor of meat and vegetables better than boiling and simmering, though admittedly they also take longer to cook. Steam cooks gently; the *Chawan-Mushi* soup of Japan, for instance, depends on a smooth custard to cook while the soup is heating in the same bowl. Then there's the advantage of not having to ladle the soup — it cooks in its own cup. This soup needs a spoon, unlike other Japanese soups, which one drinks with two hands holding the bowl.

China has an *oon joong*, a "sweat jar" with a cover for steamed soups. Beef chunks, ginger, black beans, and four cups of water are placed in the jar which has a separate tripod to stand it in the water. After five hours of steaming, four cups of liquid still remain, since there isn't any evaporation. The gently boiling water and the porous nature of the jar "sweat out" the nutrients in the meat. There's ample protein in the vitamin-rich broth. Few of these jars can be found for sale in the United States, unfortunately.

Winter Melon Bowl is another example of steamed soup. The scooped-out melon itself serves as both the cooking utensil and tureen.

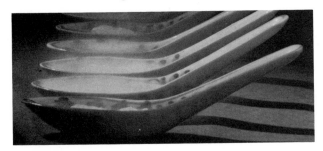

Custard Soup (Chawan Mushi)   JAPAN

⅓ cup dried shrimp
6 cups water
2 teaspoons Japanese soy sauce
¾ teaspoon salt
1 teaspoon sugar
12 fresh shrimp
6 dried mushrooms
1 teaspoon Japanese soy sauce
¼ teaspoon salt
½ *kamaboko* (steamed fish cake)
12 *fu* (dried wheat cakes)
4 spinach leaves
4 eggs

Preparation: Make *dashi* (fish soup stock) by boiling dried shrimp in water for 30 minutes. Allow to cool and season 4 cups with Japanese soy sauce, salt, and sugar. Set aside. Shell and de-vein fresh shrimp; boil them for 4 minutes in salted water. Drain, set aside. Soak mushrooms until soft, about 20 minutes. Slice, drop in ½ cup unseasoned stock, cook 5 minutes, and add 1 teaspoon Japanese soy and ¼ teaspoon salt. Set aside. Slice *kamaboko* in thin sticks. Soak *fu* for 5 minutes, squeeze dry, and slice in small slivers. Coarsely chop spinach leaves and set aside.

Assembling: Arrange boiled shrimps, mushrooms, *kamaboko*, and *fu* in 6 *chawan-mushi* dishes. Set cups on steamer tray. Break eggs into a mixing bowl, beat with a fork (do not make froth), and add 4 cups

cooled seasoned stock. Pour this mixture carefully into the bowls. Cover with *chawan-mushi* lids or aluminum foil.

Cooking: Bring the pot of water to a boil, cautiously set steaming basket in place (being careful not to knock over the little cups), cover, and steam 35 minutes over low heat until custard is set. Remove cover and lids, add spinach, cover and steam 5 minutes longer. Serve with a spoon as the first course of a meal.

Yield: 6 servings.

Variations: Numerous ingredients can go into *chawan-mushi* — shredded raw chicken, raw fish, fried fish pieces, bamboo shoots, peas, bean sprouts.

Substitute utensils: If you are not using a steamer, place bowls in a large saucepan, pour in 1½ inches of water, cover, and steam 25 minutes or until custard is set. *Chawan-mushi* dishes are slender tea cups with overlapping lids. Coffee mugs covered with foil and rice bowls covered with foil make less dainty serving dishes but hold more; the recipe could then be either a side dish or a main course.

Custom: Children snack on *chawan-mushi* at birthday parties; they even assemble their own ingredients. Babies can digest this mild-flavored custard. Adults enjoy it as a soup.

Winter Melon Bowl   CHINA
(Doan Gwa Tong)

   1 5-6 pound winter melon, about 9 inches high and 8 inches wide or a 5-6 pound half of a melon
   1 whole bamboo shoot tip
   2 tablespoons dried lotus seeds
   8 red dates (jujubes)
   5 forest mushrooms
   ¼ cup raw chicken
   7 cups of chicken stock
   2 pork chop bones
   1 teaspoon salt
   ½ teaspoon white pepper
   ¼ cup cooked smoked ham
   1 stalk green onion

Preparation: Scrub the white powder from melon. If using a whole one, cut off 2-3 inches from the top. Save to dice for the soup. Remove pulp and seeds, discard. With a sharp knife cut the rim with saw-toothed V's, like the lid to a Jack O' Lantern. Someone artistically inclined can carve dates, names, figures (dragons, birds, clouds, mountain scenery) on the melon itself. The chef at a first-class Chinese restaurant will add these designs to melon bowls for banquets. Select a heatproof bowl (at least 3 inches high) that fits the bottom of the melon and set the melon on this.

Cooking: Bring 2½ inches of water to a boil in the pot of a steamer. Place the bowl and the melon into the water; if the water spills into the bowl, reduce the water. Cover with domed lid and boil for 2-3 hours, checking the water every half hour and filling with boiling water from the kettle when necessary. The melon cooks through until all the white meat appears translucent. While the melon is steaming, dice the lid, cutting away the tough green skin. Set aside. Dice bamboo shoots into the size of peas. Set aside. Soak dried lotus seeds, forest mushrooms, and red dates in water 30 minutes. Halve dates to remove seeds. Thinly slice mushrooms into ⅛-inch pieces. Shred chicken into 1-inch threads. Set aside. Heat stock and pork chop bones in a pot for ½ hour. Skim froth off the surface, remove bones. Add winter melon, lotus seeds, mushrooms, dates, bamboo shoots, chicken, salt, and pepper. Simmer 1 hour. Bring to a boil before pouring into winter melon tureen. Dice cooked ham and shred green onions into 1-inch pieces. Set aside to use as garnish.

Assembling soup bowl: Carefully lift bowl and melon from pot, fill three-fourths full with hot soup. Sprinkle green onions and diced ham over surface. Bring melon to table with bowl underneath to keep the melon steady while serving. Whoever ladles the soup should scrape some melon flesh from the sides of the melon bowl for each guest.

Yield: 10 servings.

Serving suggestion: Use as a first course of a seven- or eight-course banquet when the melon bowl is served too. For a less elaborate entrance and an equally delicious soup, cut melon into chunks without the skin or cubes without the skin and cook with soup stock. (The skin is not eaten.) You may cook soup in the melon itself though it is very heavy to lift from the pot to the table without spilling.

Comment: Smithfield/Virginia ham has always been recommended for Chinese dishes because its smoked flavor comes close to the flavor of Chinese ham. In regions of the South and Southwest where professional pit-barbecuing produces similar results, you don't have to buy a whole ham. Buy a ham sandwich, throw away the bread, and use the ham. Any other smoked ham is good, too — it adds color as much as flavor.

rice, bread, noodles & eggs

The typical Oriental meal includes rice, or bread, or noodles — in other words, at least one food high in starch. (Of course, a banquet might serve all three dishes.) Asians eat rice everyday, either for the main course (as in India) or for a side dish (as in China). When steaming rice, soak it overnight, drain it, and cover it with 1 inch of water in a bowl deep enough to allow for its expansion. Cook in a covered steamer for 1 to 2 hours. Because steaming rice takes so long, most Orientals simply boil the rice and steam-cook it the last 20 minutes. It's easy to reheat left-over rice: put it in a bowl and place it in the steamer at least 10 minutes. Better yet, just include it in the steamer to cook with the other dishes and forget about it until dinner time.

In north India, pan-fried breads rather than rice dominate the meal. The Chinese steam white bread filled with meats and sweets for light meals and snacks. So popular is this Chinese *bao* that Thailand adapted it with a Southeast Asian filling. The same dough can be steamed (without the filling) to serve with Chinese boned roast duck slices, which the guest sandwiches within the bread bun.

Steamed noodles are another Chinese favorite. Since only a few Oriental markets stock the highly perishable rice-flour noodles, many home cooks use cake flour to obtain superb noodles that are easy to make.

Children are especially fond of *gai cheng tea* — eight-inch white noodles rolled with bits of meat and green onions. When I was a girl, I sometimes sprinkled sugar on them. Whenever my mother visits San Francisco's Chinatown, she still buys several of these large noodles for me to eat at home. Serve all noodle dishes sliced-up; they make finger-food appetizers, snacks, or side dishes.

Boiled White Rice

1 cup long-grain white rice
1½ cups water

Preparation: Rinse rice several times in water to rid it of excess starch. Drain. Cover with 1½ cups water and soak at least 15 minutes or longer. If soaked overnight, change the water the next day. The soaking softens the grain and cooks the rice faster since the water steams from inside the core.

Cooking: Boil uncovered until most of the water has evaporated or cooked in, about 5 minutes. The surface should have a few bubbles coming out of holes and the sides of the rice pot. Cover and turn heat to simmer and steam 10 minutes. Remove from burner and let rest 10 minutes before serving. Stir with a spoon and scoop rice out.

Yield: 3 cups cooked rice.

Comments: Your rice should be soft and without a hard center and your pan should have a thin crust or no crust at all. However, Koreans and Chinese like a crust at the bottom of the pot. They use a low setting instead of the lowest one to brown the rice at the bottom. The cook then scoops out the loose rice, returns the pot with the crust to the burner, and turns the heat to high. As the rice crackles and browns 1 minute the cook pours in boiling water. The water separates the crust from the pan. Family members serve themselves by breaking the crust in pieces to put in bowls with some rice water. This makes a refreshing soup at the end of a meal. My grandmother and father like to mash a boiled sweet potato with the softened browned rice to make a dessert.

Variation: If you prefer medium or short-grain rice, use equal amounts of water and rice and cook as instructed above. Long-grain rice stays drier, so the grains soak up the mouth-watering juices and sauces of Malaysian, Indonesian, Thai, Vietnamese, Chinese, Sri Lankan, and Burmese dishes.

Shorter-grain rice cooks stickier and softer. It is preferred by the Japanese, Cambodians, Laotians (who only eat sweet rice), and Koreans. Steaming rice in a steamer takes an hour. I cook rice in a pot and then reheat what is left over in a steamer. Make enough rice for two meals and heat the second portion in a bowl or plate set on a steaming rack. Cook covered 20 minutes.

Boiled Brown Rice

    1 cup brown rice
    2 cups water

Preparation: If rice was not bought in bulk, do not rinse rice. If weighed from a large container, however, rinse rice several times in water to remove impurities. Drain. Cover with 2 cups water and soak at least 30 minutes. (Brown rice takes longer to soften and cook than white rice.)

Cooking: Bring rice to a boil, lower heat to medium and cook uncovered 35 minutes or until most of the water has evaporated. Use a spoon to push aside the rice to check the bottom of the pot — if rice grains are not separate, cook longer. Cover, turn heat to low and cook 20 minutes. Remove from burner and let it rest 10 minutes. Stir before serving.

Yield: 3 cups cooked rice.

Notes: To reheat brown rice, place amount in a small bowl to steam while other dishes are cooking. It doesn't overcook. Brown rice varies — some grains are harder than others and need an extra cup of water to cook; other grains are like white rice and need ½ cup less. Orientals like white rice because it is bland and doesn't mask the different flavors of sauces during meals. Brown rice's distinct taste and chewy texture change the perceptions of sauces. A growing number of Americans prefer brown rice for daily meals (more nuitritious and more filling, so one eats less) and serve polished white rice at parties.

Steamed Buns with filling   CHINA (Bao)

Dough:
    5 pounds flour
    1 cup shortening, not butter or margarine
    2¼ cups sugar
    1½ tablespoons dried yeast
    ¾ cup warm water
    4 cups water or milk
    2 teaspoons *gon suey* (potassium carbonate solution)
    2 teaspoons vinegar

Preparation: All ingredients should be at room temperature. Heat milk to lukewarm. Mix flour and sugar. With your finger crumble and cut shortening into the flour. Add yeast to warm water, cover, and let stand 10 minutes (over a warm stove or the central pilot light, if possible). Form a well in the dry ingredients and slowly pour in the yeast mixture and water, kneading the dough as you add the liquid. Knead 40 minutes or until dough is smooth and elastic. Add extra flour if the dough is sticky, extra water if it's dry. Cover with damp cloth or lid. Let it double in size overnight. Remove lid, rub *gon suey* over the hard air-dried surface of the risen dough. Spread vinegar over dough. Let rest 5 minutes, pick off top inch of dough and knead until smooth, about 15 minutes. Return dough to large mass and knead together for 20 minutes or until texture is uniform. Let rise 2 hours.

Wrapping: To fill bun, pull off about a 2-inch ball, roll it lightly in your hand, and flatten the edges with your fingers. Place a teaspoon of filling in the center and pinch the opening closed. Lay on a 3-inch square of parchment or white butcher paper.

Decorations: The end of a chopstick dipped into a cotton ball with a few drops of food coloring will code your *baos* as to their fillings: one dot (peanut), two dots (pork), three dots (chicken), four dots (red beans), one square, two squares, and so on. When decorating remember that the Chinese like clusters in design; they never place three dots in a row. Instead, they make a three-leaf clover on each. An apricot pit sawed crosswise and filed smooth makes a pretty design, as does a chopstick that has been split one inch into four sections and divided with toothpicks.

Steaming: Place *bao* directly on aluminum or bamboo racks over boiling water. Steam 17 minutes.

Remove. Serve warm or at room temperature. **Notes:** This recipe with the pork filling originated with my Aunt King Oy of Drew, Mississippi. She, my Grandmother Moy, and I spent two afternoons making *bao*. We needed that many people to knead the dough which filled a 20-inch mixing bowl. My aunt often makes 70 *baos,* taking several dozen to New Orleans for friends, and giving many to visitors. Extra *baos* are refrigerated up to a week, then steamed 10 minutes to heat.

Yield: 6 dozen.

Fillings for Bao:
Pork Filling

> 4 pounds pork shoulder roast or tenderloin
> 3 tablespoons soy sauce
> 3 tablespoons *hoisin* sauce
> 1 tablespoon *mien see* (bean sauce)
> 2 teaspoons salt
> 3 tablespoons ketchup
> 3 tablespoons honey
> 3 tablespoons 100 proof whiskey
> garlic powder
> 2 tablespoons *nam yue* (red bean curd)

Preparation: Rinse pork with water and place in a colander to drain 20 minutes. Cut pork into 1-inch thick slices lengthwise. Marinate in soy sauce, *hoisin* sauce, *mien see,* salt, ketchup, honey and whiskey.

Cooking: Squeeze each strip to "harden" it for baking. Arrange on a rack. Bake in a 375° oven 1 hour. Turn once and sprinkle garlic powder over meat. The pork should be salty for this filling. Remove pork, allow to cool before dicing in ½-inch cubes. Remove most of the fat but leave some in — Chinese like the contrast of soft fat and firm pork; otherwise they feel it's "dry." Heat a wok, add 2 tablespoons of oil and 1 teaspoon of salt, stir-fry pork 1 minute. Add *nam yue* and cook one more minute. Remove and allow to cool. Fill *bao* and steam as directed.

Yield: 6 cups.

Leftovers: Pork filling can be used to flavor steamed or stir-fried vegetables. Add it at the end to heat; it doesn't need any more cooking.

Sweet Peanut Filling

½ cup roasted unsalted peanuts
⅓ cup shredded coconut
2 teaspoons brown sugar
1 teaspoon white sugar

Preparation: Crush roasted peanuts with a rolling pin or chop coarsely with a cleaver. In a small bowl, combine peanuts, shredded coconut, brown sugar, and white sugar. Mix thoroughly. Store in a glass jar or plastic bag until ready to use.

Yield: 1 cup.

Filling: Estimate how many buns you want to be "sweet" and measure a teaspoon for each in a bowl. Add a teaspoon of water to mix the sugars. Fill *bao*. Steam as directed.

Chicken and Mushroom Filling

1 cup raw chicken (white meat)
½ teaspoon salt
1 tablespoon port wine
2 teaspoons cornstarch
4 medium-sized dried mushrooms
1 stalk celery
2 tablespoons oil
2 cloves garlic
½ teaspoon sesame oil

Preparation: Dice chicken meat into ½-inch pieces. Marinate in salt, port, and cornstarch. Soak dried mushrooms in water 30 minutes. Stem and cut into ¼-inch thick slices, 1 inch long. Set aside. Dice celery in ½-inch cubes. Set aside. In a wok, heat oil and brown garlic. Discard garlic. Stir-fry chicken, mushrooms, and celery until the chicken is cooked, about 2 minutes. Add sesame oil, toss to mix, remove. When cool, fill *bao* with one or two teaspoons of chicken. Steam as directed.

Yield: 2 cups.

Leftovers: Lay chicken mixture over a pot of cooked rice for 20 minutes.

Serving Custom: The custom of dining on pastries at mid-day is known as "drinking tea," *yum cha.* But actually more food is eaten than tea is drunk. *Bao* is the featured item at Chinese teahouses in the San Francisco Chinatown; customers judge the quality of a teahouse-restaurant by how light and white its steamed buns are. Weekend-morning brunchers and working people on their lunch breaks fill the streets and restaurants of Chinatown from 10 to 3 every day. Other *dim sum* — some steamed, some fried — include crispy fried taro cakes, steamed shrimp balls, baked egg custard tarts, gelatine cakes, and sesame-seed puffs. If you're still hungry, you can order noodles with meat. The expense of each dish is determined by how many plates it sits on — a one-plate dish costs a certain price, a two-plate dish costs twice as much. At the end of the meal a waiter comes to your table to add up the number of plates on your table and compute your bill.

Variation: Steamed buns can be reheated by baking at 350° for 10 minutes; then the dish is called "oven *bao*," completely different from its original steamed counterpart. The color becomes golden and the texture resembles baked bread, crisp on the outside.

Red-bean Filling. It's the same as *azuki* filling in *manju*. The Chinese call it *dow saw*.

Possibilities: Steam dough without filling to make bread for a meal as a change from rice. Making *bao* can be a group project: I remember social gatherings in cities of the San Joaquin Valley when both men and women participated alike in preparing steamed pork buns, bamboo-wrapped sweet rice, and grass jelly, a Chinese gelatine dessert. We'd eat a lot, yet have enough left over for everyone to take several items home to enjoy over the next few days.

Quick Steamed Buns (Bao)   CHINA

    1 cup lukewarm tap water
    ½ teaspoon sugar
    1 package dried yeast
    1 cup water
    1 cup sugar
    5 cups self-rising flour (Wondra)
    ½ teaspon vinegar
    2 egg whites
    1 teaspoon white shortening
    parchment or white paper

Preparation: Have all ingredients and utensils at room temperature. Mix water and ½ teaspoon sugar in a bowl. Add yeast. Use a toothpick to stir yeast to the bottom of the bowl. Cover and set on the pilot light of a stove or in a warm area. Dissolve 1 cup sugar in water with about 5 minutes of stirring. Set aside. Shape flour into a mound on a large cookie sheet. Make a well, pour in yeast mixture slowly as you use a metal spoon to dissolve the flour in the water. Add vinegar and egg whites in the same manner. Continue stirring until it's too thick to stir. Add shortening and ¾ cup of sugar-water mixture and knead 20 minutes. Now cover the sticky mass with a large bowl and move it with the cookie sheet to a warm area for an hour to rise. Cut 24 3-inch squares from parchment or white paper.

Wrapping: Remove bowl from risen dough. Put ½ cup flour in a cup to use if dough is hard to handle. Grease hands with white shortening and take a 2-inch section of dough. If it's sticky, roll it in the flour. Now massage the flour into the ball, using little pressure. You can handle the dough a lot, but always use a light touch or else it won't rise properly. With your fingers, work the ball into a small pancake. Place a teaspoon of filling in the center and close the opening by pinching the sides together. A dab of shortening seals it. Place seam side down on paper squares.

Decoration: Dip seven thin straws tied together in a ball of cotton damp with food coloring and touch each *bao*. *Voilà!* You have a chrysanthemum flower design. In China, cooks used reeds instead of these paper straws.

Cooking: Set decorated buns in steaming cage. Wait 20 minutes for dough to rise. Bring water to a boil, place rack on steamer pot, cover, and steam 15 minutes. Serve warm or at room temperature.

Yield: 2 dozen.

Toasted Coconut Filling

½ cup canned toasted coconut
3 tablespoons sesame seeds
5 teaspoons sugar

Combine all ingredients to fill 1 recipe Quick Steamed Buns. The filling tastes like crunchy candy.

Yield: 1 cup.

Pork Filling (Salapaw)   THAILAND

1 cup raw pork
2 dried mushrooms
8 water chestnuts
1 small onion
3 stalks coriander
1 teaspoon sugar
2 tablespoons oil
3 hard-boiled eggs

Preparation: Mince pork. Set aside. Soak dried mushrooms in water 30 minutes, dice in ¼-inch pieces, combine with pork. Coarsely chop water chestnuts. Chop onion in ½-inch chunks. Shell eggs (saving the egg whites for another dish) to obtain yolks.

Cooking: In a wok, heat oil and stir-fry all ingredients except egg yolks until pork loses pink color. Remove and allow to cool. Crumble egg yolks and sprinkle over cooled pork mixture. Fill 24 buns and steam as directed.

Yield: 2 cups.

Rolled Noodle (Gai Cheng Tea)   CHINA

2 stalks green onions
3 tablespoons dried shrimp
1 cup cake flour (Swansdown)
2 teaspoons cornstarch
2 tablespoons oil
1¼ cup water

Preparation: Shred green onion finely. Soften dried shrimp by soaking in tap water for 30 minutes. Chop and set aside.

Making noodle: In a medium-sized bowl, sift flour and add cornstarch. Stir in oil with a metal spoon. Gradually add water, stirring constantly to dissolve flour in water. (Batter becomes smooth and lump-free.) Set aside. Oil four 10-inch glass pie plates or 8-inch metal pie plates.

Steaming: Bring a pot of water to boil, set oiled pie plate on steaming rack, measure ½ cup batter, and pour it over plate, covering all gaps with a film of white. Sprinkle slivered green onions and chopped shrimp over this noodle. Cover. Steam 3-5 minutes until the noodle is transparent. Bubbles will form while it cooks; these disappear when the noodle cools. Remove plate and allow to cool. Repeat with another plate until all batter is used. To remove noodle, use the back of a spoon to loosen the top edge of the noodle. Roll the noodle with the spoon and your fingers. Transfer to a serving platter.

Yield: 4 rolls. Cut into 2-inch sections. Serve as a finger-food snack, an appetizer, or a side dish.

Variation: Bits of cooked meats and vegetables rolled in the noodle make the dish even tastier.

Cooking hint: A 4-inch-high four-legged trivet set in the middle of a steamer pot of boiling water allows you to pick up the pie plate to move the batter around to cover its bottom.

EGGS: EASY SIDE DISHES

Steamed eggs, like steamed meat patties, fill out Southeast Asian and Chinese menus with side dishes that are easy to make. The eggs themselves are bland, so different ingredients vary the flavor of the recipes tremendously. There are secrets to a smooth custard: add boiled water that has cooled to the eggs, use a thick bowl to encourage slow cooking, and keep the water boiling gently.

Smooth Egg　　　CHINA

    4 medium-sized eggs
    ¼ teaspoon salt
    1 cup water
    8 dried shrimps
    1 small pork chop
    1 tablespoon light soy sauce

Preparation: Break eggs into a deep bowl. (Save egg shells to measure water.) Beat slightly. Add salt. Set aside. Bring water to a boil and allow to cool. Set

aside. Soak shrimp in tap water for 20 minutes. Set aside. Mince pork. With your fingers, make tiny meatballs and drop into eggs. Drain shrimp and add to eggs, too. Measure an equal amount of cooled water to eggs using the egg shells as a guide. Stir gently until water and eggs are mixed well.

Cooking: Over medium boiling water (i.e., water brought to a boil and then its heat lowered until water is bubbling softly), set dish on steaming rack. Steam 15 minutes or until eggs are set. Retrieve. Drizzle soy over surface. Serve warm or at room temperature.

Yield: 4 small servings.

Serving suggestion: Plan this mild side dish with its custard texture with any cuisine and other methods of cooking. Increase the number of eggs for more servings and use a larger bowl to accommodate the increased liquid.

Cooking hint: Eggs steamed over vigorously boiling water lose their smooth surface and feel hard. If you have other dishes to steam, cook the eggs first, remove, and steam the others over rapidly boiling water. The dish and eggs remain warm several minutes.

Variation: Omit shrimp and pork, substitute ¼ cup of canned clams. Add 1 tablespoon light soy sauce to custard before steaming.

Peppercorn Eggs　　　THAILAND

    6 medium-sized eggs
    2 cups water
    2 tablespoons milk
    ¼ teaspoon pepper
    ⅛ teaspoon garlic powder

1 teaspoon soy sauce
1 teaspoon Szechwan peppercorns
Garnish:
2 cloves garlic

Preparation: Boil water and allow to cool. In a medium-sized soup bowl, break and beat eggs to mix the white and yolk without creating a froth. Use egg shells to measure 6 shells of cooled water to the eggs. Stir in milk, pepper, garlic powder, and soy sauce. Crush Szechwan peppercorns with mortar and pestle or the wooden handle of a knife; add to eggs.

Steaming: Bring a pot of water to boil, reduce heat for a gentle boil, set bowl on rack, cover, and steam 15 minutes or until eggs are set. While eggs are cooking, mince garlic and fry in a little oil.

Serving: Retrieve eggs. Garnish with fried garlic bits. Serve warm.

Yield: 4 servings.

Eggs with Coriander   VIETNAM

6 medium-sized eggs
2 cups water
2 dried mushrooms
3 stalks fresh coriander
1 stalk green onion
½ cup cooked crab meat
1 teaspoon salt
¼ teaspoon pepper
Chili-and-Garlic Sauce:
1 red chili
1 clove garlic
1 tablespoon fish sauce
½ teaspoon sugar
2 teaspoons vinegar
2 teaspoons lime juice

Preparataion: Boil water and allow to cool. In a medium-sized soup bowl, break and beat eggs. (Do not make froth.) Using the 6 egg shells, measure an equal amount of water into the beaten eggs. Set aside. Soak dried mushrooms in tap water 20 minutes or until soft. Stem, slice thinly, and add to eggs. Mince fresh coriander and green onion. Mix with eggs. Flake crab meat over eggs. Stir in salt and pepper.

Steaming: Bring a pot of water to boil, then lower heat to keep the water boiling slightly. Set dish on rack, cover, and steam 15 minutes or until eggs are set. While eggs are cooking, make chili-and-garlic sauce. Finely mince red chili and garlic. Place in a small bowl. Stir in fish sauce, sugar, vinegar, and lime juice.

Serving: Retrieve eggs. Either sprinkle chili-and-garlic sauce over eggs or serve it as a dip. This recipe stays warm 20 minutes, though it's also delicious at room temperature.

Yield: 4 servings.

desserts ~ happy endings

Oriental desserts seem bland to some Westerners. Asians generally prefer a smooth texture instead of a chewy one, a light taste instead of a syrupy one, a subtle flavor instead of a sweet one. The Red Bean-Filled Bun of Japan is a good example of what Asians enjoy as a treat. Steamed cakes are light confections that stay moist for days. Apples and pears, steamed and then chilled, make elegant desserts. But for a grand ending to a meal, Almond Cream comes closest to the richer delicacies eaten in Occidental countries, though the Oriental smooth texture persists.

Golden Glow Pears   CHINA

4 ripe or nearly ripe yellow pears
honey

Preparation: Cut off the top of each pear (leave stalk intact). Core the pears with a small knife and a ¼ teaspoon measure. Pour honey into the hollow until three-fourths full — the pear juices will fill the rest during steaming. Cover with conical pear top. Set in a deep plate with one cup of water.

Cooking: Place pan on steaming rack. Steam in a covered pot for 25 minutes. Retrieve. Serve warm in individual bowls.

Yield: 4 servings.

Cooking hint: If the pear doesn't stand upright, slice a quarter inch off the bottom to even its base. Don't overcook the pears or they will be mushy. Chinese pears are a smaller, spherical variety with green skins and firmer flesh like an apple.

Variation: Cream or half and half added to the last inch of the pear before serving is a non-Oriental but delicious touch. Raisins and dried fruits steamed in the honey make a holiday treat.

Variation: Sweet Chilled Pears. 1 teaspoon powdered sugar; coffee or mint liqueurs. Core pears as in Golden Glow Pears. Fill each fruit with ¼ teaspoon of powdered sugar, cover with pear top, and set in a deep pie pan filled with a cup of water. Steam covered for 25 minutes. Remove, take off pear tops, pour a tablespoon liqueur in each well. Allow to cool before capping pears and chilling them for two hours.

Serving suggestion: Bring out pears in decorated dishes and serve with coffee.

Variation: Steamed Pears. Carve initials, designs, stripes on pears. Make a solution of 1 cup water and 2 tablespoons brown sugar. Stand pears in a deep dish and pour sugared water over pears. Steam covered 30 minutes. Serve warm. The brown sugar colors the white designs of the pears. Food coloring and white sugar do the same (instead of brown sugar). A simple, nutritious dessert.

Empress Apples   CHINA
(Ping Gwoh)

6 Golden Delicious apples or any other available apples

Preparation: Wash and core apples with a small

knife and ¼ teaspoon measure. Set in a deep pie pan.

Cooking: Bring water to a boil, place pan on platform, cover, steam 25 minutes. Retrieve. (Juice oozes into pan; save this and refrigerate it for a refreshing summertime drink, or else drink it warm on a cold day.) The steamed fruit is tender but not pulpy. Serve either chilled by itself or warm and filled with cream or ice cream.

Yield: 6 apples.

Variations: 1) Fill with honey, cinammon, and chopped nuts before steaming. 2) Fill with red bean paste before steaming.

Advantages of steaming: Steaming apples instead of baking them guarantees a firm juicy dessert; the apple needs no basting, since it doesn't dry out as it would when oven-baked. If your Red Delicious apples are crisp, just eat them raw. Steaming a soft apple improves its flavor and texture, but nothing can add to the goodness of a perfect eating apple.

Red Bean-Filled Bun (Manju)   JAPAN

Filling:
> 2 cups *azuki* (red beans)
> water
> 1½ cups sugar
> ½ teaspoon salt

Preparation: Soak *azuki* overnight in water to soften skins. Drain, put in a large pot, and cover with at least three inches of water. Boil for 1½ hours, replacing water as necessary to keep beans from sticking. Stir occasionally. Drain and pulverize the *azuki* in small batches with a blender (not all the skins will disappear and this adds texture and color to the filling). Cook the beans on medium heat, slowly adding the sugar and salt. When the sugar and salt have dissolved, cook 10 minutes longer on low heat, stirring constantly. Let cool. Refrigerate overnight if you have time.

Dough:
> 3 cups flour, not sifted
> 4 teaspoons baking powder
> 1¼ cups sugar
> 1 teaspoon salt
> ½ teaspoon powdered green tea
> 3 eggs
> 1 tablespoon milk
> ½ teaspoon vanilla
> ½ cup oil

Preparation: Mix together flour, baking powder, sugar, salt, and green tea. Set aside. Beat eggs, milk, and vanilla. Add oil to wet ingredients. Make a well in the dry ingredients and slowly stir in egg mixture. Knead about 25 minutes into a smooth dough "as soft as your ear lobe" (say the Japanese). If possible, refrigerate the dough overnight to make it firm and easier to handle.

Wrapping: Take a 1½-inch section of dough, roll and press lightly in your palm. Then with your fingers flatten the edges of the circle leaving a slight bump in the center. Spoon a teaspoon of *azuki*, place it on top of the bump, and pinch the ends together to form a ball. Rest with seam side down.

Steaming: Bring a pot of water to boil. Line the steamer baskets with a damp cotton cloth. Let the steam heat the cloth for 10 minutes. Set the *manju* about two inches apart to allow for expansion. Steam covered 20 minutes and remove the balls before the cloth dries. Serve *manju* warm or at room temperature.

Yield: 3 dozen.

Variations: Adjust the amount of sugar for the *azuki* to suit your taste. Orientals don't like syrupy treats and use as little as ¾ cup; double or triple the measurement for a sweet tooth. Fresh filling can be frozen and used without thawing. Canned *azuki* has a smoother consistency and makes an excellent substitute. Store in a glass jar in the refrigerator; it'll last for months. Refrigerate extra dough up to three weeks. Reheat chilled *manju* in the steamer 10 minutes.

The green tea imparts a light green color and pleasant bite to the *manju*; cinnamon, tumeric, and paprika flavor and color the dough, too. Food coloring added to different batches creates a rainbow of colorful balls.

Serving custom: On Girls' Day, March 3, Japanese girls visit each others' homes to admire elaborate and decorated hand-made dolls. Hostesses offer snacks of *manju*, *senbei* (assorted crackers), and jelly-type candies. This centuries-old custom is celebrated with pink and white colors throughout the cities, towns, and homes to honor the girls. Japanese likewise enjoy *manjus* at birthday parties and festive occasions.

Rice Cakes (Puto) PHILIPPINES

1 cup rice flour
1 cup whole wheat flour
4 teaspoons baking powder
½ teaspoon salt
1 cup sugar
1 cup milk
cupcake liners

Garnish:
fresh coconut crumbs

Preparation: In a large mixing bowl combine rice flour and whole wheat flour. Add baking powder, salt, and sugar. Stir with a metal spoon as you pour in milk. Continue stirring until dry ingredients dissolve and no lumps remain. Set aside. Line 12 individual cupcake tins. Spoon batter to half-fill containers. Set on both steaming trays.

Steaming: Bring a pot of water to boil in steamer pot, place baskets over water, cover, and steam 30-35 minutes until done — stick a toothpick in the center of a cupcake. If it comes out clean, remove trays.

Serving: Retrieve fluffy cakes out of tray and tins. Sprinkle with coconut crumbs. Serve warm with tea or coffee.

Yield: 12 cupcakes.

Variation: Can be buttered for dinner rolls. Reduce sugar by ¼ to ½ for less sweet taste.

Custom: Filipinos have adopted Western — especially Spanish — dining habits. They eat later meals than other Asian countries and their *puto* makes a delicious snack before a late dinner around 7 or 8. Its sweetness and pretty petaled surface of tiny cracks gains approval for it as a dessert also. If a cake is desired, pour batter into a lightly oiled angel food cake tin and steam 30-35 minutes.

Almond Cream   CHINA
(Ai Toy Go)

1 quart whole milk
1 quart half and half
2 sticks agar-agar
1½ cups sugar
7 teaspoons almond extract

Preparation: Into a large saucepan (more than 3 quarts), pour milk and half and half. Break sticks of agar-agar into 1-inch pieces or smaller and drop into pot. Stir and let soak 1 hour.

Cooking: Turn heat to medium and cook mixture 10 minutes to dissolve agar (a gentle boil helps). Add sugar and stir to dissolve. Do not use wooden utensils. Before adding almond extract, ladle a cup of cream through a sieve — little or none of the agar should be seen; otherwise the mixture must boil longer to dissolve the agar. After this test, return the cup of cream to the saucepan. Remove from heat, stir in the almond flavoring and blend with the cream. Strain through a sieve into a dry mold, pan, or bowl. Allow to cool. Refrigerate two hours to chill while it thickens. Serve only when firm.

Yield: 1 10-inch square.

Serving ideas: Here's an ideal dessert for any meal, informal or formal. This is one of the richest desserts in any Chinese cuisine. Scoop out the velvet-smooth contents with a spoon or cut into squares and serve. Small ice cubes placed in each bowl help maintain a cool temperature. The cook may add fresh or canned fruits — oranges, peaches,

lichees, strawberries, mandarin oranges, watermelon balls, cantaloupe slices — to each serving bowl for variety. My source for this recipe is Herman Quan of Fresno, California.

Cooking hint: Instead of boiling the milk (which may scorch it), dry steam it in a double boiler.

Banana Variation: Flavor the dessert with 7 teaspoons of banana extract instead of almond extract; the results taste exotically Polynesian. For other variations, substitute strawberry or vanilla extract flavorings.

Egg Cake   CHINA
(Gai Don Go)

1 cup cake flour (swansdown)
8 medium eggs
1 cup sugar
3 tablespoons fresh lemon juice

Preparation: Line bottom of cake pan with parchment paper. Set aside. All ingredients should be at room temperature. Sift flour twice. Set aside. Separate egg whites and egg yolks into two separate large bowls. Beat egg whites at high speed until soft peaks form, about 10 minutes. Carefully add 2 tablespoons of sugar. Beat thoroughly. Repeat until sugar is used up and egg whites are stiff. Set aside. Add lemon juice to egg yolks, beat to a light yellow color. Fold yolks into whites — be careful not to break many air bubbles. Now fold flour into mixture, three tablespoons at a time until well blended. Try not to disturb mixture more than necessary. Pour batter into cake pan.

Yield: 1 9-inch square cake or 1 round angel food-shaped cake

Cooking: Bring water to a boil, lower heat until water boils gently. Place cake pan on platform, cover, steam 30 minutes. Retrieve, remove paper, slice, and serve warm or cold.

Comments: This egg cake is a true "sponge" cake; its texture depends on the amount of air beaten into the egg whites and yolks and the care in which the flour is folded in to give the cake lightness and height. The cake needs no leavening agent. Any jarring motion when the cake is removed causes it to fall. This moist and tempting steamed confection with its delicate yellow color and fresh fragrance keeps well for a few days, either covered on the table or refrigerated. It doesn't dry out as fast as a baked cake. Sweets like Egg Cake were originally steamed instead of baked, since ovens were not part of most Chinese kitchens. If such sweets are not available, the Chinese eat fresh fruits or drink another soup at the end of a meal.

Additional idea: It's delicious as a side dish with Vietnamese Cellophane-Noodle Fish.

New Year Cake   CHINA
(Fot Go)

      Paper cup cake liners
      1 cup packed brown sugar
      1 cup water
      1⅓ cups buttermilk baking mix (Bisquick)
      1⅓ cups flour (Swansdown)

Garnish:
      Sesame seeds

Preparation: Place twelve paper liners in individual tart tins. Dissolve brown sugar in water with 5 minutes of stirring with a metal spoon. Set aside. Combine baking mix and flour in a large bowl. As

you pour the brown sugar mixture into flour, stir with the metal spoon to make a batter with no lumps. Fill each tin half-full and place on steaming tray.

Cooking: Bring water to a vigorous boil, set rack over water, cover, and steam 25 minutes without peeking. Retrieve; sprinkle sesame seeds while the cakes are hot. Serve warm or at room temperature. The light brown cake rises and splits into an "open mouth laugh" appropriate for all good times.

Yield: 1 dozen cupcakes.

Making metal cups: If you cannot purchase separate custard cups or baking tins for this recipe, improvise. I saw my aunt, Ethel Chin of Fresno, California, take a twelve-cup muffin tin and cut out the shells with a pair of metal cutters and then smooth the edges with a file.

Custom: New Year Cakes are always made into cupcakes for good luck. Only happy families make these to celebrate the new year. It's a dessert comparable to pumpkin pie at Thanksgiving.

THE ACCOMMODATING COCONUT

Inhabitants of Asia depended on the coconut for "milk," oil, and food; they used the coconut palm fronds for roofs, leaves for clothing, the shells of empty coconuts for bowls, the halved coconut as a steaming vessel, and the green husks that cover a young coconut for spoons.

The coconut needs a stand to keep it upright; its natural shape causes it to roll over. Natives use two large dark green *ti* leaves to twist into a holder. Lay two leaves stem to stem with one leaf halfway covering the other. Twist one over another until the stems are not visible. Knot into a circle, large enough for a coconut; the two pointed ends look like the ends of a bow tie. Nothing is as authentic and colorful on the table as a fibrous rough-looking brown coconut (filled with water or fruit) in a cool, glossy, green setting.

Fresh Coconut Milk

1 coconut
2 cups boiling water

Preparation: Choose a coconut with some juice inside — shake it to feel the liquid sloshing around. With the dull side of a knife blade scrape away dirt and stringy covering (otherwise these get into the coconut meat after you crack the nut). A hammer and screwdriver easily open the coconut. There are three soft spots noticeable at one end. Pierce two or three of these with the screwdriver; a hammer helps. The liquid that flows out is coconut juice and may be drunk as a refreshment. Drip into a glass, chill, and drink later — or, if you prefer, simply discard the liquid. Before cracking the coconut, lay some paper towels over newspapers on the kitchen floor. Hold the coconut in your hand and tap sharply with the hammer around the circumference of the nut, rotating it as you proceed. Continue until you hear a different sound, a hollow thud — this means you've located and enlarged a crackline. Place the coconut on the paper towels and give it a solid blow at this precise spot. When the halves fall apart you will be surprised at the purity of white displayed by the coconut meat. It doesn't resemble the canned coconut or packaged coconut from the supermarket. It's faintly sweet, not grainy and sugary; chewy and crisp, not soggy; and moist, not hard. Here is a flavor that cannot be duplicated, so try to use fresh coconut whenever possible.

Milking a coconut: A small knife and a little patience scrapes out a cup or more of coconut meat sliver by sliver. Place these in a blender, pour in 2 cups of boiling water, and whip for 10 seconds. Then start the blender again and increase the speed to "liquefy" for 60 seconds. You may use the milk as is — the "cream" will rise to the top (this is also known as "thick milk" and is used for making desserts and thickening the curries of Southeast Asia and India).

Unfortunately the coconut cream from one coconut won't make a dessert. Frozen coconut milk mixed with fresh coconut milk substitutes almost as well. The "thin milk" under the cream is used for thinning curries. Refrigerate milk in a covered bottle to use for up to five days.

Yield: 2-3 cups.

Additional ideas: For fresh coconut meat, pour the milk through a fine sieve, squeezing as much liquid out of the coconut powder as possible. The coconut can be frozen for instant availability. The milk will be thinner but can still be used for curries when combined with dairy milk. Some people put the coconut halves in a 300° oven for 20 minutes to loosen the flesh, then crack the coconut shell again and cut out the meat, but I find the coconut loses its fresh taste with this expedient. Oven heat is a last resort with an older coconut, one that doesn't have as much liquid inside and whose meat is tougher to scrape.

THAILAND
Sweet Coconut Pudding (Khanom Talai)

> 1 cup thick coconut milk, fresh if possible
> 2 tablespoons rice flour
> 3 tablespoons light brown sugar
> aluminum foil

Preparation: Divide the coconut milk in two portions, add 1 tablespoon of flour to each. Mix until blended. To one portion, stir in the brown sugar; this will be the bottom layer of the coconut cup. Set aside.

Making Cups: Cut 15 3½-inch circles of aluminum foil. With one circle, make four pleats, each pleat an equal distance from the other, to form a cup (no

toothpicks are needed to hold its shape). Set all holders on a deep dish about ½ inch apart. Measure 2 teaspoons of the brown sugar mixture into each cup.

Steaming: Bring the water to a boil, set plate on rack, cover, and steam for 20 minutes. Uncover. Wear an oven mitt to measure one teaspoon of coconut milk and rice flour mixture into each cup. Cover and steam 20 minutes longer. Retrieve and transfer to another dish. Serve at room temperature.

Yield: 15 tiny cups.

Coconut Uses: The Thais often employ rose water instead of water to extract the coconut milk. They make banana-leaf holders for the pudding. Coconut sweets are popular everywhere in Asia, though they aren't always steamed. The Hawaiian *haupia* (coconut pudding) thickens at room temperature with cornstarch; Cambodians and Laotians cook bananas in coconut milk; the Chinese fill steamed buns with coconut shreds and peanuts.

Leftovers: When made in aluminum cups, the coconut pudding doesn't refrigerate well. It's better to steam the cups and allow to cool before serving.

Variation: To one cup of coconut milk, add three beaten eggs and three tablespoons brown sugar. Mix well and pour into a seeded small pumpkin or acorn squash. Set on a plate over boiling water, cover, and steam 1 hour. Chill. Slice into wedges and serve. This is *Sankhaya* — the favorite custard dessert of the Thais.

Glossary of Ingredients

AGAR-AGAR: Made from seaweed to thicken sauces, desserts, puddings. Sold as white powder and 1-inch sticks in Oriental groceries. Lasts 6 months in an airtight container.

AJINOMOTO: See *Monosodium Glutamate.*

AZUKI: See *Red Bean Paste.*

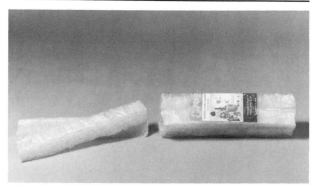

BAMBOO LEAVES, DRIED: Purchased in bundles from Oriental markets. Soak 4 hours or overnight to soften leaves — they are water repellent when dry. Excellent for steaming fish. Also popular: wrap glutinous rice and meat in them to boil for 3 hours. Leaves can be scraped clean, rinsed, and reused until they crack.

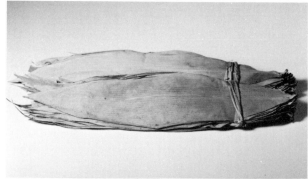

BAMBOO SHOOTS: Available fresh or water-packed in cans. The whole bamboo shoot tips are suitable for dicing and slicing into triangular shapes. The sliced bamboo shoots require no extra cutting unless slivers are needed. Fresh bamboo shoots taste sweeter; peel off the green husk of several layers, then slice. Store fresh and canned leftovers in water. Cover. Change water daily and the shoots will last two weeks.

BANANAS, COOKING: Firmer (vegetable) variety than the banana fruit eaten raw. Fry without the skin if green. Boil and steam if ripe. Different varieties come from Costa Rica and Hawaii — some shaped more like a potato than the familiar curved shape. Green bananas will ripen in one to two weeks.

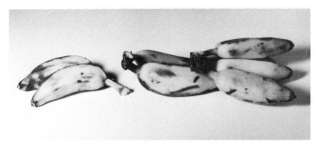

BANANA LEAVES, FRESH: Sold in frozen packages in Oriental markets. One leaf is three feet long — cut what you need and return the rest to the freezer. Thawed repeatedly, the leaves become brittle. The smell of steamed banana leaves is sweet — the food takes on a light, fresh taste.

BASMATI RICE: Long-grain rice preferred for Indian dishes. Available in Oriental groceries.

BEAN CURD, FRESH: Sold in individual plastic tubs covered with cellophane. Sometimes labeled as *dow fu* or *tofu.* Buy creamy colored cakes (avoid the yellow old ones) in single blocks which are soft and best for soups, or else as four slices of the firm and all-purpose variety. Cover and store in water in the refrigerator. Change the water daily. Good for six days.

BEAN CURD, RED *(Nam Yue):* Salty pungent fermented bean cake (the red color is introduced). Sold in square tins in Oriental markets. If you wish to avoid food coloring, substitute the less flavorful but colorless Fermented Bean Curd, sold in glass jars. Transfer canned contents to a clean jar and refrigerate. It remains usable for several months.

BEAN SAUCE: Sold as "Yellow Bean Sauce" and "Ground Bean Sauce"; also known as brown bean sauce or *mien see* (Chinese). This canned or bottled fermented soy bean product is found in many Oriental grocery stores. Refrigerates in air-tight jars for up to several months.

BITTER MELON (*Balsam Pear*): The quinine content of the vegetable imparts its cooling bitter flavor. Can be eaten when as small as three inches or as large as eight. Halve and seed. Stir-fry, steam, or blanch as the Filipinos do for a salad. Its bumpy exterior, a light green to dark green color, is a welcome sight to foreign-born Chinese in the United States.

BLACK BEANS, FERMENTED AND SALTED (*Dow See*): A Chinese spice. Small raisin-size black beans sold in plastic or cellophane packages. May be rinsed and mashed with minced garlic and ginger for steaming, stir-frying, and braising. Keep them at room temperature or refrigerate in an air-tight container.

BOK CHOY: See *Chinese Chard.*

CELLOPHANE NOODLES: See *Noodles, Dried Mung Bean.*

CHILI OIL: Purchased in bottles in Oriental markets. Flavor comes from pressed chilies.

CHILI PEPPERS, GREEN: Mexican Jalapeño variety is widely available in the United States. Longer, thinner green chilies of Southeast Asia are sometimes grown locally by Asian-Americans who sell them to Oriental groceries. If these peppers are obtainable, grind dozens of them in the blender and store in a covered glass jar in the refrigerator. They then last indefinitely.

CHILI PEPPERS, RED: Southeast Asian varieties can be shaped like peas or long, thin green chilies. The round chilies are considerably hotter than the green ones. Purchase fresh or in bottles as a chili sauce.

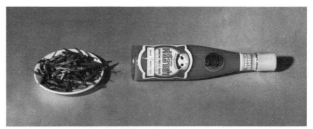

CHILI PEPPERS, RED, DRIED: Sold in cellophane packages in some supermarkets, Mexican groceries, and Oriental markets. A convenient substitute for fresh chilies. Soak to soften and either mash for sauce or chop for stir-frying.

CHINESE CHARD *(Bok Choy):* White stalks and large dark green leaves characterize this vitamin-rich vegetable. The Chinese peel away the stalks of the leaves to get its heart — *choy sum* — for special occasion meals. Use within the week. Sold in Oriental groceries and some supermarkets.

CHINESE EGGPLANT: A small variety of eggplant, more diminutive than the variety sold in supermarkets. Sometimes shaped like conventional eggplants, sometimes almost ball-shaped. The purple skin is very tender, so it doesn't have to be peeled before cooking. Buy in Oriental groceries. Use within two weeks.

CHINESE SAUSAGE *(Lop Cheong):* A fatty pork sausage sold in Oriental groceries. Mild flavored. Keep refrigerated or frozen. Cook before eating.

COCONUT CREAM: The thick layer that rises to the top of fresh coconut milk. Use for desserts. Supplement with frozen or canned coconut milk if insufficient cream is present. See *Fresh Coconut Milk* (pp. 79-80).

CORIANDER, FRESH (*Chinese Parsley, Cilantro*): The herb's leaves and stalks are used in all Asian countries; Thais use its roots, too. Can be a garnish for any dish (usually for fish and chicken). Often chopped and added to a minced meat dish. Its sharp taste disappears and its delicate leaves wilt in a few days; use soon after purchase.

CORIANDER, GROUND: Spice employed in curries and minced meat dishes. Sold in bulk or purchased in bottles. Store in air-tight can. Lasts indefinitely. Most Indian households roast the coriander seeds (along with other spices) and then grind them to make each meal's fresh curry.

CUMIN: An indispensable spice used in Indian curry-making. Bought in bulk, in bottles or cans. Store in air-tight containers for years.

CURRY: Made from a variety of spices, including (for Indian curries) tumeric, cumin, coriander, cinammon, and cardamon. Southeast Asian curries contain some of those spices as well as lemon grass, garlic, and chili powder. Both versions use coconut cream to thicken and coconut milk to thin the curries.

CURRY PASTE, RED (*Keang Som*): Thailand's curry paste for seafood and fish. Usually can be purchased in small plastic envelopes in Oriental groceries. Contains "dry chili, onion, salt, kaphi, kachai, grass," according to its list of ingredients. Store in air-tight container. Lasts one year, though it gradually loses its potent flavor.

DOW SAH: See *Red Bean Paste.*

DRIED FOREST MUSHROOMS: See *Mushrooms, Dried.*

DRIED MUSHROOMS: See *Mushrooms, Dried.*

DRIED SHRIMP: See *Shrimp, Dried.*

FISH SAUCE: Used like soy sauce in Southeast Asia. Gives off a strong fishy smell in the bottle, but when blended with chilies, garlic, and vinegar it has a pleasant bite that is uniquely Southeast Asian. Produced by draining the juice of fish packed in wooden crates. Vietnamese fish sauces have a stronger taste than the Thai, Burmese, or Philippine ones.

FU: Dried, pressed wheat cakes to be soaked, squeezed dry, and sliced in Japanese Chicken Rice. Store in air-tight containers. Purchase in Oriental markets.

GARAM MASALA: An Indian spice borrowing some flavoring from curry making, but not cooked as long, if at all. Stirred in at the end of a curry stew, *garam masala* may be purchased in bottles and bags or made at home. See p. 33 for a recipe.

GHEE: Clarified butter originally made from buffalo milk. Removing the milk solids from butter allows it to withstand high temperatures; consequently it can be stored without refrigeration. Lends a distinctly "Indian" flavor to foods. See p. 33 for more information.

GINGER, FRESH: Its hot taste and color is essential to Oriental cooking. Buy the less wrinkled roots, since they will last longer. If the climate is humid, scrub root clean, allow to dry, and store in the inside shelf of refrigerator door. Otherwise, leave on the open shelf to remind you to use ginger frequently to flavor foods. If ginger is scarce, peel it and place in a jar of sherry in the refrigerator; it'll last a year. Or grate and freeze it; do not freeze whole.

GLUTINOUS RICE: Short-grain rice used for desserts and leaf-wrapped snacks. Its grains stick together after cooking. A common item in most Oriental markets. Does not have a "shelf life" as long as white long-grain rice.

GON SUEY: A potassium carbonate solution used to tenderize meat. In this book, it is used with vinegar to soften the air-hardened surface of risen dough. Available in bottles from Oriental groceries. Simply store on shelf.

GREEN TEA, POWDERED: Used in tea ceremonies of Japan, but also as both food coloring and flavor in *manju,* a red-bean filled dessert. Lasts indefinitely. Flavors and colors ice cream, too.

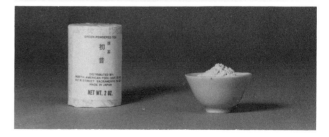

HOISIN SAUCE: Thick sauce that looks like chocolate topping. Smokey flavor resembles barbecue sauce of the American Southwest. Made from soybeans, sugar, vinegar, fermented rice, chilies, and spices. Most Oriental markets stock *hoisin* sauce. At home, refrigerate it in an air-tight glass jar.

HOT BEAN SAUCE: Made from long red chilies and bean sauce. Buy in cans or jars. Refrigerate in glass jar for up to 1 year. Substitute in place of bean sauce for spicier recipes.

JUJUBES: See *Red Dates.*

KAMABOKO: Steamed fish cake for Japanese recipes. Sold frozen in Oriental markets. Thaw and use for as long as 1 week. It becomes sweet tasting when cooked.

KANPYO: Dried vegetable gourd strips used in Japanese cooking. Soak, then cook until transparent, season, and use in making vinegared rice rolled in seaweed (*norimaki sushi*).

KEANG SOM: See *Curry Paste, Red.*

KONNYAKU: Yam noodle cake used in Japanese cooking. Slice into thin pieces and cook.

LILY BUDS, DRIED: Soak in water 20-30 minutes until soft; cut off tough end and tie in knots or chop. Add to any steamed Chinese dish. Sold in plastic bags or cellophane-wrapped cakes. The lighter the color of the lotus flower buds, the better the taste. Store in air-tight containers on the shelf.

LOTUS SEEDS, DRIED: Light-colored seeds that must be soaked in water and then cooked several hours to soften. Store indefinitely without refrigeration.

MIEN SEE: See *Bean Sauce*.

MIRIN: Sweet rice wine for cooking Japanese dishes. Buy in bottles from Oriental groceries. Lasts indefinitely.

MISO: Soybean paste used in Japanese soups and vegetables. Red miso is saltier than white miso and is therefore preferred by most Japanese. Sold in cans or plastic tubs in the refrigerated section of Oriental speciality markets.

MUSHROOMS, DRIED: Flat, dried, brown-colored mushrooms that must be soaked in water before use. These are less expensive than the forest mushrooms, which have a curled edge and a pattern on their tops. Forest mushrooms are smaller, thicker, and juicier than flat dried mushrooms but forest mushrooms are so expensive they are used only in party dishes. Store at room temperature in an air-tight container.

NAM YUE: See *Bean Curd, Red*.

NOODLES, DRIED MUNG BEAN: Thin, brittle dried noodles. Also known as "cellophane noodles," sometimes sold as *saifun*. Soak in water to soften before using for steamed or stir-fried dishes. Drop dry in hot oil for a puffy noodle to garnish salads. Purchase in Oriental markets in packages of 2 oz. or more. Store in air-tight container. These noodles last for years.

NORI: Dried sheets of seaweed for Japanese *norimaki sushi* (vinegared rice rolled in seaweed). Toast *nori* over low heat to remove moisture before rolling *sushi*. If possible store in an air-tight container. Lasts 1 year. The Japanese prefer the stronger taste of the darker-colored sheets.

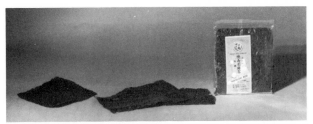

OYSTER SAUCE: Made from oysters and soy sauce. Smooth brown sauce with a distinctive flavor. The only possible substitute for oyster sauce is additional soy sauce. Purchase oyster sauce in Oriental shops and certain supermarkets. Refrigerate or store in a cool place.

PLANTAINS: See *Bananas, Cooking.*

RED BEAN CURD: See *Bean Curd, Red.*

RED BEAN PASTE: Small round red beans rich in vitamin A are soaked, boiled, and sweetened with sugar to make a paste as a filling for steamed bread *(bao)*. Sold by weight in plastic bags. Store in air-tight container at room temperature. Fresh bean paste can be frozen and used without thawing. Canned bean paste, which is extremely sweet-tasting, should be stored in an air-tight glass jar in the refrigerator; it lasts for months if you avoid dripping water into the paste when you use part of it.

RED DATES: Sweet dried red dates. Soak in water, halve to remove seed, and use in soups and steamed dishes. Buy in plastic bags. Store in air-tight containers on the shelf.

RICE FLOUR: Finely ground white rice. Stores indefinitely without refrigeration. Available in health food stores and Oriental markets.

RICE VINEGAR: A white vinegar distilled from rice. Resembles ordinary white vinegar, which is an excellent substitute. Purchase rice vinegar in Oriental grocery markets. Store on the shelf.

SAKÉ: Japanese rice wine used for cooking and drinking. Substitute dry sherry if necessary.

SALTED EGG *(Hom Don):* Duck or chicken eggs that have been pickled in a salt solution or preserved in an ash covering. Purchase individually in Oriental markets. Scrape off black coating, if necessary, rinse, and crack — the egg white is still a jelly liquid but the yolk has "petrified" into a clear orange ball. Use in minced meat dishes.

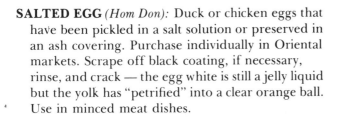

SALTED FISH: Sold dried or in cans and jars. Rinse and cut a small piece to steam as a side dish, or shred a few pieces to place atop minced meat dishes. Buy in Oriental grocery stores.

SESAME SEED PASTE: Ground sesame seeds in a thick paste. Available in cans or jars. Kept cool, it lasts for years.

SHALLOTS: Purple onions of Asia. Crispy when fried. Sometimes available in speciality groceries and supermarkets. Substitute white or yellow onions.

SHORT-GRAIN RICE: The Japanese favor this type of rice. Use it to make *sushi*. Oriental groceries stock it in bags of various sizes. Short-grain rice cooks fluffier than the long-grain variety.

SHRIMP, DRIED: Salty, chewy shrimp that must be soaked before using. Can be boiled for stock, chopped and added to flavor vegetables, or mixed into any steamed dish. Purchase in plastic bags. An expensive item, but a small amount suffices for several dishes. Store in container on pantry shelf.

SHRIMP PASTE, DRIED: Strong-smelling brown paste made from salted shrimp. An essential flavoring for Southeast Asian cooking. Purchase in plastic jars in Oriental groceries. Stores on the shelf indefinitely.

SOY SAUCE: A dark brown liquid made from soybeans, sugar, salt, and flour. Indispensable to Oriental cooking. Light or thin soy tastes salty; dark or black soy has a stronger yet somewhat sweeter flavor. Japanese soy sauce is milder and lighter-colored than Chinese soy sauce. Every country has its own brands that impart distinctly different flavors to recipes. Purchase in markets, Oriental groceries, and specialty stores. It is now possible to buy a low-salt (8%) soy sauce that's considerably milder than ordinary varieties. Store on shelf or refrigerate up to six months.

STAR ANISE, DRIED: Star-shaped seed that imparts a licorice flavor. Add whole to soups and stews; roast and grind before adding to rice powder as a spice. Store on pantry shelf in air-tight container.

SUDARE: Mat of wooden sticks for rolling the seaweed sheets in *norimaki sushi*. Purchase these disposable mats in Oriental markets. Discard when the sticks start to leave fine sawdust on food; it's then time to buy a new *sudare*.

SWEET RICE: See *Glutinous Rice*.

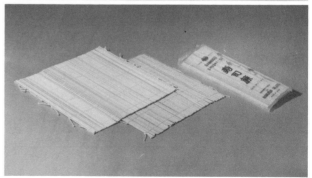

SZECHWAN PEPPERCORNS: Licorice-tasting seeds that must be crushed before using. Buy in small packages and store indefinitely in an air-tight container.

SZECHWAN TURNIP, PRESERVED *(Jar Choy):* Chinese vegetable known as "mustard pickle"; occasionally sold as "preserved radish." Canned in a red chili-powder liquid. Rinse before using. Refrigerate unrinsed portion up to three months in an air-tight jar. Chop in small pieces and add to steamed meats.

TEA MELON: Sold as "sweet cucumber," this small, delicate, squash-like vegetable comes canned. Can be eaten without cooking or can be cooked atop minced meat dishes. Store in air-tight jar in the refrigerator.

TERIYAKI SAUCE: A variety of Japanese soy sauce. Purchase in markets and Oriental groceries. Store on the shelf. Makes a sweet marinade for meats.

TI LEAVES, FRESH: Abundant in Polynesia, this useful leaf serves as dishes and as a wrap for food. In the United States, florists often order them from San Francisco where they are imported from Hawaii. Peel the stiff stem from the underside of a leaf before wrapping foods.

TOFU: See *Bean Curd, Fresh.*

TUMERIC: A golden-colored spice that is used in India and Southeast Asia to flavor curries and other dishes. Purchase in bulk, cans, or bottles in grocery stores. Tumeric will color foods — especially fish — a dazzling yellow. (Beware of touching counter tops or cloth with tumeric — it stains effectively.)

TURNIPS, PRESERVED *(Choong Choy):* A Chinese vegetable preserved in salt and bought in plastic bags. Rinse before using. Functions like the Preserved Szechwan Turnip to give texture and flavor to minced meat dishes. Not as spicy as the Szechwan cabbage. Refrigerate un-rinsed vegetable in wrapped plastic for three months.

WASABI POWDER: Often called "Japanese horseradish." The spice imparts hot flavor as a dip for shrimp, *sushi* and chicken. Mix with water to make a consistency like a mustard. Purchase in cans from Oriental grocery markets. Lasts indefinitely.

WATER CHESTNUT POWDER: Available in small boxes from Oriental stores. After opening, transfer to air-tight can. The pulverized, dried, water chestnuts look like either fine powder or peebly white sand; coarser-grained powder gives a crispier texture to deep fried meats.

WATER CHESTNUTS: Fresh water chestnuts are covered with a brown skin. Peel to prepare the crunchy fiber that can be added to any dish. Canned chestnuts are ready to use. Refrigerate unused chestnuts in water. Change water daily up to a week.

WINTER MELON: A frosted green melon shaped like a watermelon but practically hollow inside, and therefore much lighter in weight. All sizes. The larger melons have a richer, more desirable flavor. Buy whole or in a chunk sold by weight. Wash off white coating, open, remove seeds, and slice or dice into pieces for soup. The tough skin is not eaten, though it can be cooked along with its flesh. Diners can peel it away as they drink the soup. The longer the melon cooks, the more flavorful the stock becomes, though after three hours it can get too strong for most palates. Cover the exposed surfaces of any extra melon with plastic wrap to refrigerate it for several weeks. My mother and grandmother often kept their backyard harvest of melons in our cool garage for six months to a year at a time.

WON TON WRAPPERS: Highly perishable fresh noodles. Buy these frozen whenever possible. Refrigerate a few days or re-freeze (noodles thawed a second time may stick together if the cornstarch between each sheet has dissolved into a gooey paste).

YARD BEANS: A delicious, dark green, thin vegetable, named for its extraordinary length. Use in Oriental dishes, whether steamed, stir-fried, or boiled. Buy in season in most Oriental markets. Substitute green beans if necessary.

Index of Recipes

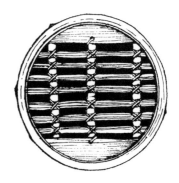

ACKNOWLEDGEMENTS

For recipes and suggestions I am grateful to Hisako Tsuchiyama Roberts, Driftwood, Texas; Jean Wong, Fresno, California; Sheila Lee Hancock, Austin, Texas; Machiko Netsu, Austin, Texas; King Oy Chin, Drew, Mississippi; Ethel Chin, Fresno, California; Pat Teepatiganond, Austin, Texas; Herman Quan, Fresno, California; Katherine Wong, Fresno, California; Chai Damrong, Austin, Texas; Byoung Baek, Austin, Texas; Shigeko and Otis Burnie, Austin, Texas; Tamie Tsuchiyama, Austin, Texas. Jeanne Flattery of Berkeley, California typed the manuscript. Alan Gribben of Austin, Texas sampled the recipes and edited my manuscript.

NOTES:

OTHER BOOKS BY TAYLOR & NG:

WOKCRAFT by Charles & Violet Schafer. An authoritative and entertaining book on the art of Chinese wok cookery. Authentic, easy to follow recipes for beginners and professionals alike. Illustrated by Win Ng.

RICECRAFT. Authoress Margaret Gin delves into the fact, fiction and fancy of rice. A collection of inventive recipes takes full advantage of the international versatility of rice. Fanciful illustrations by Win Ng.

TEACRAFT — a treasury of romance, rituals, and recipes. A book of tea — its multiplicity of uses and varieties, how to test and taste, plus recipes to complement teatime. Written by Charles & Violet Schafer, illustrated by Win Ng.

BREADCRAFT by Charles & Violet Schafer. A connoisseur's collection of bread recipes: what bread is, how you make it, and how you can create your own bread style. Plus a chapter devoted to breadspreads! Illustrated by Barney Wan.

PLANTCRAFT by Janet Cox. A practical and fun guide to indoor plant care. Illustrated charts depict the growing characteristics and conditions for over 60 plant varieties. Photo gallery by L. C. Spaulding Taylor.

HERBCRAFT by Violet Schafer. The mystery of herbs unveiled: 87 pages describe 26 herbs — their origin, history, use, growing and storing conditions. Illustrated by Win Ng.

COFFEE. The story behind your morning cup: Charles & Violet Schafer elaborate on coffee — its origin, many varieties, how to brew it and what to brew it in. With recipes for companion foods. Illustrations and photography by Alan Wood.

CHINESE VILLAGE COOKBOOK. Authoress Rhoda Yee tells her story — all about the wok and wok cookery, coupled with colorful narratives on everyday life in a Chinese village. A stir fry chart, photographic food glossary and authentic recipes guide the novice to wok mastery in no time!

DR. TERRI McGINNIS' DOG & CAT GOOD FOOD BOOK. Authoress Terri McGinnis, veterinarian and pet expert, unravels fact from fiction in this up to date, clear, concise, and convenient guide to pet nutrition: what to look for in commercial foods, how to cook up your own at home, how to recognize and feed special needs. Illustrated by Margaret Choi.

DIM SUM. Rhoda Yee teaches how to prepare a Chinese Tea Lunch at home! Explicit recipes for preparing the traditional delicasies with a chapter on suggested menus make *dim sum* easy and exciting to do. Photographic.